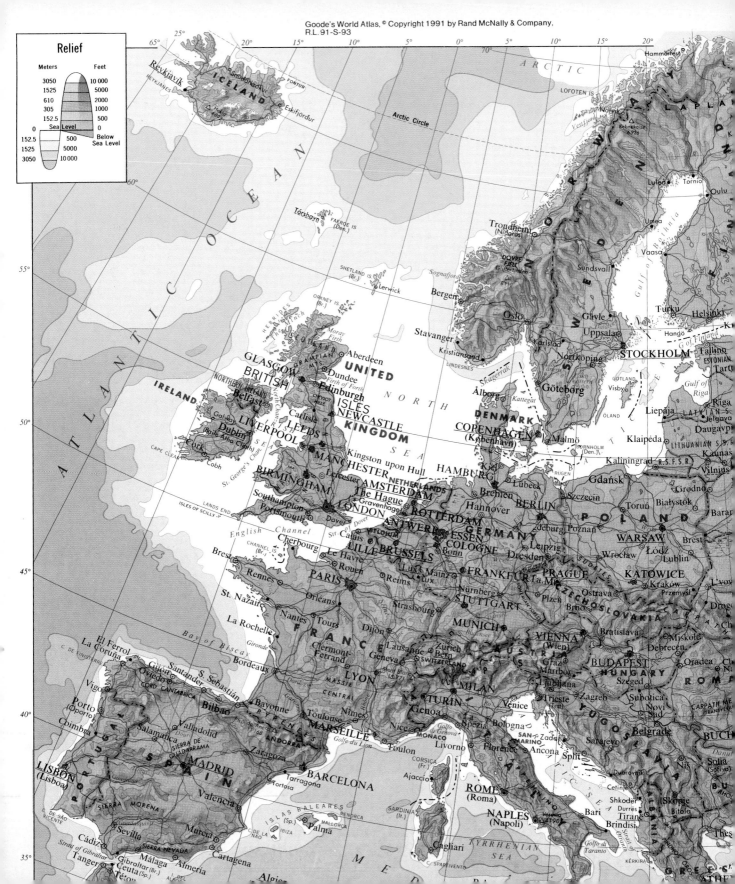

NORTH SEA

FRISIAN ISLANDS

NETHERLANDS

GERMANY

MECKLENBURG

NIEDERSACHSEN

NORDRHEIN-WESTFALEN

HESSEN

THÜRINGEN

SACHSEN

BAYERN (BAVARIA)

WÜRTEMBERG

BADEN

PFALZ

SAARLAND

RHEINLAND-PFALZ

FRANCE

SWITZERLAND

AUSTRIA

OBERÖSTERREICH

SALZBURG

KÄRNTEN

TIROL

VORARLBERG

LIECHTENSTEIN

ČECHY (BOHEMIA)

BOHEMIAN FOREST

POMERANIA (POMMERN)

Cities and towns:

Kiel, Kiel Bay, Flensburg, Eckernförde, Husum, Heide, Neumünster, Itzehoe, Bad Oldesloe, Elmshorn, HAMBURG, Lübeck, Lübecker Bucht, Wismar, Rostock, Stralsund, Rügen, Greifswald, Barth, Demmin, Güstrow, Schwerin, Parchim, Ludwigslust, Neubrandenburg, Pasewalk, Ueckermünde, Anklam, Wolgast, Szczecin (Stettin), Goleniów, Stargard Sz., Gryfino, Pyrzyce, Choszczno, Kamień Pomorski, Trzebiatów, Kołobrzeg, Gorzów

Cuxhaven, Bremerhaven, Bremen, Delmenhorst, Oldenburg, Papenburg, Emden, Leer, Wilhelmshaven, Norden, Norderney, Wangerooge, Borkum, Ameland, Terschelling, Vlieland, Texel, Den Helder, Alkmaar, AMSTERDAM, Utrecht, Zwolle, Deventer, Apeldoorn, Enschede, Almelo, Hengelo, Gronau, Nordhorn, Lingen, Meppen, Nienburg, Verden, Soltau, Uelzen, Lüneburg, Lüneburger Heide, Celle, Wolfsburg, Stendal, Gardelegen, Salzwedel, Wittenberge, Perleberg, Pritzwalk, Neustrelitz, Waren, Müritz, Röbel, Templin, Prenzlau, Zehdenick, Neu Ruppin, Oranienburg, Eberswalde, Bad Freienwalde, Bernau, BERLIN, Potsdam, Brandenburg, Rathenow, Genthin, Magdeburg, Schönebeck, Zerbst, Dessau, Bitterfeld, Wittenberg, Lübben, Cottbus, Forst, Spremberg, Senftenberg, Frankfurt an der Oder, Fürstenwalde, Strausberg, Eisenhüttenstadt, Wilhelm-Pieck-Stadt Guben, Zielona Góra, Żary, Żagań, Zielona

Groningen, Leeuwarden, Emden, Osnabrück, Minden, Hannover, Braunschweig, Helmstedt, Haldensleben, Bielefeld, Herford, Detmold, Hameln, Hildesheim, Wolfenbüttel, Goslar, Halberstadt, Quedlinburg, Bernburg, Aschersleben, Stassfurt, Köthen, Münster, Gütersloh, Paderborn, Lippstadt, Soest, Hamm, Ahlen, Einbeck, Northeim, Göttingen, Nordhausen, Eisleben, Halle, Merseburg, Leipzig, Delitzsch, Eilenburg, Wurzen, Riesa, Grossenhain, Meissen, Dresden, Bautzen, Görlitz, Jelenia Góra, Kamenz, Löbau, Zittau, Liberec, Arnhem, Nijmegen, 's-Hertogenbosch, Tilburg, Eindhoven, Kleve, Gladbeck, Bottrop, Gelsenkirchen, ESSEN, Dortmund, Hagen, Wuppertal, Solingen, Duisburg, DÜSSELDORF, Mönchengladbach, Gummersbach, Siegen, Kassel, Heiligenstadt, Mühlhausen, Sondershausen, Sangerhausen, Naumburg, Weissenfels, Zeitz, Gera, Altenburg, Grimma, Döbeln, Mittweida, Karl-Marx-Stadt, Freiberg, Pirna, Sebnitz, Decin, Ústí nad Labem, Ceská Lípa, Mladá Boleslav, Turnov, Jablonec nad Nisou, Trutnov

COLOGNE (Köln), Aachen, Bonn, Siegburg, Gummersbach, Marburg an der Lahn, Bad Hersfeld, Eschwege, Eisenach, Gotha, Erfurt, Weimar, Jena, Arnstadt, Suhl, Meiningen, Zella-Mehlis, Schmalkalden, Saalfeld, Rudolstadt, Greiz, Crimmitschau, Glauchau, Zwickau, Reichenbach, Aue, Plauen, Oelsnitz, Annaberg-Buchholz, Chomutov, Most, Teplice, Litoměřice, Mělník, Kralupy, Kladno, PRAGUE (Praha), Elbe (Labe), Kolín, Chrudim, Havlíčkův Brod, Jihlava

Hückeswagen, Heinsberg, Verviers, Spa, Malmédy, Eupen, Ahrweiler, Andernach, Mayen, Neuwied, Koblenz, Limburg an der Lahn, Wetzlar, Giessen, Fulda, Hünfeld, Bad Kissingen, Hildburghausen, Coburg, Kulmbach, Hof, Neustadt b.C., Marktredwitz, Sonneberg, Bayreuth, Bamberg, Schweinfurt, Würzburg, Kitzingen, FRANKFURT AM MAIN, Wiesbaden, Mainz, Hanau, Offenbach, Aschaffenburg, Darmstadt, Bensheim, Worms, Bad Kreuznach, Bingen, Bad Dürkheim, ODENWALD, Speyer, MANNHEIM, Heidelberg, Bruchsal, Heilbronn, Schwäbisch Hall, Rothenburg, Ansbach, Fürth, Nürnberg, Schwabach, Neumarkt, Amberg, Weiden, Schwandorf, Cham, Domažlice, Klatovy, Strakonice, Písek, Tábor, České Budějovice, Třeboň, Jindřichův Hradec

Luxembourg, LUXEMBOURG, Trier, Saarburg, Saarbrücken, Saarlouis, Zweibrücken, St. Wendel, Kaiserslautern, Neustadt, Ludwigshafen, Pirmasens, Wissembourg, Karlsruhe, Rastatt, Pforzheim, Ludwigsburg, STUTTGART, Esslingen, Göppingen, Schwäbisch Gmünd, Aalen, Heidenheim, Nördlingen, Neuburg, Ingolstadt, Eichstätt, Landshut, Straubing, Regensburg, Deggendorf, Passau, Linz, Steyr, Amstetten, St. Pölten, Metz, Thionville, Sarreguemines, Sarrebourg, Saverne, Haguenau, Strasbourg, Sélestat, Colmar, Freiburg, Offenburg, Lahr, Villingen, Schwenningen, Rottweil, Schramberg, Tübingen, Reutlingen, Ulm, Neu Ulm, Memmingen, Augsburg, Dachau, Freising, MUNICH (München), Mühldorf, Braunau, Ried, Wels, Gmunden, Bad Ischl, Wolfsburg

Pont-à-Mousson, Nancy, Lunéville, Épinal, Mirecourt, Saint-Dié, Remiremont, Vesoul, Montbéliard, Belfort, Mulhouse, Guebwiller, Thann, Basel, Lörrach, Schaffhausen, Konstanz, Winterthur, Baden, Zürich, Ravensburg, Friedrichshafen, Kempten, Kaufbeuren, Weilheim, Bad Tölz, Rosenheim, Traunstein, Bad Reichenhall, Salzburg, Bischofshofen, Bad Aussee, Liezen

La Chaux-de-Fonds, Neuchâtel, Biel, Bern, Solothurn, Olten, Luzern, Sankt Gallen, Dornbirn, Bregenz, Feldkirch, Bludenz, Innsbruck, Schwaz, Kufstein, Kitzbühel, Zell am See, Spittal, Lienz, Villach, Klagenfurt, Wolfsberg, Leoben, Bruck, Kapfenberg, Mürzzuschlag, Graz, Judenburg, Knittelfeld, Donawitz, Neunkirchen, Wiener Neustadt

Lausanne, Geneva (Genève), Montreux, Sion, Martigny, Locarno, Bellinzona, Chur, Davos, St. Moritz, Sondrio, Bolzano, Bressanone, Brunico, Merano, Pieve di Cadore, Toblach, CARNIC ALPS, KARAWANKEN, HOHE TAUERN, NIEDERE TAUERN, BRENNER PASS, BERNER ALPEN, JURA, RHÄTISCHE ALPEN, Mont Blanc

Water features:
Elbe, Weser, Ems, Rhine (Rhein), Main, Neckar, Danube (Donau), Mosel, Saale, Oder, Neisse, Spree, Inn, Isar, Lech, Naab, Regen, Eger (Ohře), Vltava, Berounka, IJsselmeer, Waddenzee, Jadebusen, Kiel Canal (Nord-Ostsee-Kanal), Mittelland Kanal, Dortmund-Ems-Kanal, Schweriner See, Müritz, Bodensee, L. Geneva

54° 50° 48°

HELGOLAND

Enchantment of the World

GERMANY

By Jim Hargrove

Consultant for Germany: Bruce Murray, Ph.D., Assistant Professor of German, The University of Illinois at Chicago

Consultant for Reading: Robert L. Hillerich, Ph.D., Visiting Professor, University of South Florida; Consultant, Pinellas County Schools, Florida

CHILDRENS PRESS ®

CHICAGO

From Neuschwanstein Castle in Bavaria, one has an incredible view of the surrounding lakes and wooded mountains.

Library of Congress Cataloging-in-Publication Data

Hargrove, Jim.
    Germany / by Jim Hargrove.
       p.   cm. — (Enchantment of the world)
    Includes index.
    Summary: Describes the history, geography,
reunification, notable cities, government, and lifestyles of
Germany.
    ISBN 0-516-02601-1
    1.   Germany—Juvenile literature.   [1.   Germany.]
I.   Title.   II.   Series.
DD17.H344   1991   91-22645
943—dc20   CIP
                                                                 AC

Picture Acknowledgments
AP/Wide World Photos: 11, 23, 46 (left), 50 (right), 52 (right), 56 (2 photos), 57 (right), 58, 63 (2 photos), 65 (3 photos), 66, 68 (2 photos), 73 (right), 89, 94 (2 photos), 95
© **Cameramann International, Ltd.:** 9 (right), 28 (right), 30, 36, 75 (top), 79 (left), 80 (left), 81 (top left), 82 (2 photos), 83, 86 (left), 104 (left), 109, 112 (2 photos), 120, 124 (2 photos), 125, 127 (bottom)
© **Virginia R. Grimes:** 8 (right), 35, 46 (right), 71 (right), 72 (3 photos), 73 (center), 121 (right)
H. Armstrong Roberts: © **M. Koene,** 102 (left);
© **Camerique,** 118 (left); © **M.Burgess,** 121 (left)
Historical Pictures Service, Chicago: 8 (left and center), 55 (inset)
Journalism Services: © **Fotex,** 16 (right), 70, 75 (bottom), 119
© **Kirkendall/Spring:** 115 (left)

Lauré Communications: © **Rapho Guiliumette,** 110 (bottom left)
North Wind Picture Archives: 26, 28 (left), 33, 38, 39, 41 (left), 50 (left), 52 (left)
Chip and Rosa Maria de la Cueva Peterson: 12 (bottom left), 96 (top left, bottom left and right), 104 (right), 116, 127 (top)
Photri: 15 (right), 18 (left), 41 (right), 51, 55, 57 (left), 74 (top right), 101 (left), 102 (right), 110 (top right), 113, 118 (right); © **B. Kulik,** 122
© **Porterfield/Chickering:** 18 (right)
© **Carl Purcell:** 16 (left), 74 (left), 96 (top right)
Root Resources: © **Russel A. Kriete,** 12 (bottom right);
© **Ric Ergenbright,** 17; © **Jane H. Kriete,** 21; © **Leonard Gordon,** 87 (left); © **Kramarz,** 98, 110 (top left), 115 (right), 123 (2 photos); © **Paul Conklin,** 99; © **Vera Bradshaw,** 126 (2 photos)
Bob and Ira Spring: 15 (left), 76 (top), 85 (left)
Tom Stack & Associates: © **Hugh K. Koester,** 19;
© **Manfred Gottschalk,** 78, 87 (right), 105 (right)
SuperStock International, Inc.: 43; © **Mauritius,** Cover Inset, 107; © **Steve Vidler,** 5, 45, 86 (right); © **Karl Kummels,** 6; © **Kurt Scholz,** 9 (left), 76 (bottom); © **Eberhard Streichan,** 12 (top); © **Silvio Fiore,** 29; © **Giorgio Ricatto,** 73 (left); © **Dave Forbert,** 81 (right); **Schuster,** 84
Third coast Stock Source: © **Bryan Peterson,** 105 (left)
TSW-CLICK/Chicago: Cover, 4, 101 (right), 106; © **Andras Dancs,** 62; © **Ed Simpson,** 79 (right); © **Lois Moulton,** 80 (right); © **J. Messerschmidt,** 81 (bottom left);
© **Taubenberger,** 85 (right); © **Rick Rusing,** 110 (bottom right)
Valan: © **Aubrey Diem,** 61; © **Christine Osborne,** 71 (left), 121 (center)
© **Jim Whitmer:** 74 (bottom right)
Len W. Meents: Maps on 13, 58, 59, 69
Courtesy Flag Research Center, Winchester, Massachusetts 01890: Flag on back cover
Cover: Bavaria Ransau
Cover Inset: Congress Building, Berlin

These boys are wearing Lederhosen, *the shorts of the traditional Bavarian costumes.*

TABLE OF CONTENTS

Chapter 1

A NEW GERMANY

The Germans call their nation *Deutschland*. Located in the heart of Europe and often playing a central role in world history, it is one of the most famous countries on earth.

This is remarkable. Throughout recorded time, Germany has existed as a single, unified nation for less than a century in total. There was a unified Germany for seventy-four years from 1871 to 1945 and again during the relatively brief period from October 3, 1990 until the present. At all other times, there were at least two, and sometimes many more, German lands and German governments.

Today, a visitor to modern Germany can instantly see that German culture is far older than the unified nation's brief history. In many cities and towns, ancient churches, palaces, and castles, some dating back to the Middle Ages, stand next to gleaming steel-and-glass office buildings. At the same time, ancient forests and mountainous areas have been carefully protected so that they appear much as they must have looked a thousand years ago.

The impact of German history affects people across much of the planet today. Long before there was a single, powerful German nation, there were Germans who changed the world.

Opposite page: Old and new buildings stand alongside one another in Frankfurt, which is known for its international finance.

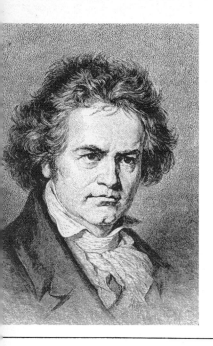

From left to right: Ludwig van Beethoven, Johannes Gutenberg, and a statue of Richard Wagner

More than five hundred years ago, during the 1450s, German printers, including Johannes Gutenberg, developed the first modern printing presses. In 1517, the German religious reformer Martin Luther began the Reformation by nailing a list of spiritual thoughts to the church door in the town of Wittenberg. The act led to the birth of the Protestant Christian church. Today, there are more than 350 million active members of Protestant churches throughout the world.

In the centuries that followed the Reformation, Germans produced some of the world's greatest art, literature, and especially, music. German composers played a pivotal role in the creation of much of the world's enduring music. Among the most famous were Bach, Handel, Beethoven, Mendelssohn, Schumann, Brahms, Mahler, Strauss, and Wagner. Mozart and Haydn came from neighboring Austria. Compositions by this handful of Germanic musicians still dominate the world of classical music.

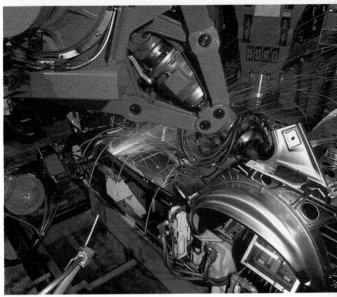

An early Volkswagen "Beetle" on the assembly line in Wolfsburg (left) and a robot welding arm in the BMW (Bavarian Motor Works) plant in Munich (above)

You don't have to love classical music to enjoy another German invention: the automobile. In 1876, the German engineer Nikolaus Otto created the first modern engine, which was based on mechanical principles still used today. Nine years later, in 1885, another German engineer, Karl Benz, built the first automobile to make successful use of Otto's engine. Not surprisingly, some of the best-known cars in the world are made in Germany today. They include luxurious models by Mercedes-Benz and Audi, and the economical Volkswagen. Certain German highways, called *Autobahnen*, are among the world's best—and fastest!

Tragically, Germany is also the nation which, in the twentieth century, brought warfare and racism to a new level of murderous cruelty. As a result of the battles of World War II, which ended in 1945, a number of German cities were completely destroyed. Today, many seemingly ancient buildings are actually meticulous reproductions of buildings destroyed by bombs during the war.

9

For about forty years following the end of World War II, the German nation was divided. For most of that time, there were two Germanys. West Germany, formally known as the Federal Republic of Germany, was an independent democracy. The German Democratic Republic, commonly called East Germany, was governed as a Communist dictatorship largely controlled by the Soviet Union. Despite its name, the German Democratic Republic was anything but a true democracy.

As the years passed, the people of democratic West Germany were able to rebuild their country after the devastation of World War II. The West German economy became one of the world's strongest. In Communist East Germany, on the other hand, people were not so fortunate. Their economy was inefficient. By the end of the 1980s, for example, there were fewer than four million privately-owned automobiles in all of East Germany. At the same time, there were about thirty million cars owned by West Germans. Many East Germans wanted to move west; most were forbidden to do so. Some were killed by soldiers and police while trying to escape.

In the middle and late 1980s, some of the differences between East and West Germany began to diminish. Largely because of changes in the Soviet Union brought about by Mikhail Gorbachev, people in East Germany were given more freedom to criticize their government. Near the end of the decade, East Germans won many more freedoms, including the right to travel with few restrictions to the West.

During a series of rapid developments in the year 1990, the two German states were reunited. On October 3, 1990, the German Democratic Republic (East Germany) officially ceased to exist. From that date on, the basic government of the Federal Republic

Celebration at Brandenburg Gate, Berlin, on the eve of German unification

of Germany (formerly known as West Germany) was extended to the entire new nation.

For all Germans, and particularly those living in former German Democratic Republic territory, unification offered the promise of a better life. But there were also many problems. In the months following unification, thousands of businesses once run by Communist officials failed. Millions of former East Germans lost their jobs or were forced to work reduced hours. Former West Germans had to pay higher taxes to support their unemployed countrymen. Huge demonstrations for higher wages were held in many German cities.

Despite the problems, the 1990s are an exciting time for Germans and Germany. A nation whose people were so often at the center of history is once again at the center of history-in-the-making.

Vineyards of Rhineland (above),
St. Bartholomä on Lake Konigssee (below
left), rolling hillscape northeast
of Stuttgart (below right)

Chapter 2

THE LAND CALLED DEUTSCHLAND

The map shows: Elbe River, North Sea, Baltic Sea, North German Plain, Berlin, Rhine River, Central Highlands, Main River, Alpine Foothills, Black Forest, Bavarian Alps.

Because it is located in the heart of Europe, Germany has many neighbors. Nations touching its western boundary are the Netherlands, Belgium, Luxembourg, and France. Switzerland and Austria are to the south; Poland and the Czech Republic to the east. Germany's northern border extends to the North Sea, to the nation of Denmark, and to the Baltic Sea as well. Its total area is 137,854 square miles (357,042 square kilometers), a little bit smaller than the state of Montana in the United States.

Like other countries in western Europe, Germany is densely populated. Approximately 81 million people lived in Germany in 1994. The rate of population increase has been gradually decreasing since the mid-1970s. As a nation, Germany has one of the lowest birth rates in the world.

VARIED LANDSCAPES

Like the people who inhabit it, the German landscape is extremely diverse. It includes open flatlands and gently rolling hills, lovely lake districts, vast river valleys, high and low mountain ranges, and large areas of forest. In general, German land is highest in the south and lowest in the north. For this reason, most rivers in Germany flow from south to north, eventually emptying into either the North Sea or the Baltic Sea. Some geographers divide the nation's terrain into four major areas: the northern plains, the central highlands, the Alpine foothills of southern Germany, and the Rhine River Valley.

THE NORTHERN PLAINS

Northern Germany, along the coasts of the North and Baltic seas, is low and relatively flat. A small area near the eastern border has rolling hills running parallel to the Baltic seacoast. In both the North and Baltic seas, groups of islands dot the coast, most close to the German mainland. Some of the islands are popular vacation spots.

In northwestern Germany, huge dikes, or seawalls, protect the land from North Sea floods. It is not an easy task. Part of the Atlantic Ocean, the North Sea has periodic tides that cause its level to rise and fall. When a high tide is accompanied by stormy weather, a frequent occurrence around the North Sea, only large, well-made dikes can keep the sea from covering huge areas of land.

Coastal waters in both the North and Baltic seas are generally quite shallow. Most large German harbors, therefore, are located near the mouths of rivers leading into the sea. Here, the water is deep enough for oceangoing ships to come close to the shore. Man-made canals connect virtually all of Germany's major rivers. The canals make it possible to ship goods throughout much of the country.

Thousands of years ago, the low-lying plains of northern

Hamburg (left) is Germany's publishing center; Berlin (right) is the capital.

Germany were covered by glaciers. The flatlands, lakes, and gently rolling hills were sculpted by the great sheets of ice. The flat, relatively fertile land was ideal for farming. But not all of this area is farmland and pasture fields. The two largest cities in Germany, Berlin and Hamburg, are located in the northern plains.

THE CENTRAL HIGHLANDS

The plains of northern Germany extend southward irregularly into an area of ancient mountain ranges sometimes called the central highlands. These hills were once higher and sharper than they are today. Over millions of years, they were worn down by water and wind erosion.

The Black Forest (left) covers 106 miles (170 kilometers). Unfortunately some growth is being threatened by acid rain, fire, and other environmental pollution (above).

Despite their age, the highlands of central Germany are rugged and picturesque. Travel in this area was once quite difficult. But today, modern roads crisscross the highlands, following river valleys and mountain passes. Many of the hills and plateaus, some created by ancient volcanoes, are covered with dense forests. The Bohemian Forest is located along Germany's border with the Czech Republic. The famous Black Forest, although considered part of the central highlands, is really in southeastern Germany. Named for the dense growth of trees that nearly block all sunlight, the Black Forest is another popular German vacation area. Forests cover about one-third of Germany's total area.

Unfortunately, air and water pollution threaten the health of all of Germany's great forests. Some scientists fear that many of the trees in Germany, and other European countries as well, are gradually dying. During the 1980s, Germany joined other European nations in taking the first serious steps to diminish environmental pollution.

Parts of the Zugspitze are skiable and the summit can be reached by several cableways.

More than a dozen mountain ranges rise up throughout the central highlands. Some of the best known are the Harz Mountains, which rise abruptly out of the northern lowlands, and the mountains of the Black and Bohemian forests.

THE ALPINE FOOTHILLS

A small section of Europe's most famous mountains, the Alps, extends into the state of Bavaria in southern Germany. Bavaria is the largest of Germany's sixteen states. But the part of Bavaria that can boast of true Alpine mountains is really quite small. More of the area is taken up by smaller foothills of the Alps. Nevertheless, one of the tallest of all the Alpine peaks, Zugspitze, is located in Bavaria. With a height of 9,721 feet (2,963 meters), Zugspitze is Germany's highest mountain.

As mountains go, the Alps are relatively young. They have sharp, snowcapped peaks, deep valleys, and swift mountain

A typical Bavarian landscape and traditional house

streams. The Bavarian Alps, as Germany's small but rugged part
of the mountain chain is called, is the most popular vacationland
in the nation. It is easy to see why. The scenery, in both summer
and winter, is breathtaking. Much of the land seems to have come
alive from a fairy tale. Gingerbread houses (really made of wood)
have steep roofs to allow snow to slide off. In the summer, the
same houses often have window boxes filled with colorful
flowers. The jagged Alpine peaks are a background for the exotic
old castles and churches that dot the countryside.

Located near Zugspitze, the twin Bavarian towns of Garmisch
and Partenkirchen make up one of Europe's best-known winter
ski resorts. During the frosty winter months, skiers by the
thousands can be seen gliding down the steep slopes of Zugspitze.

The Zugspitze forms a backdrop for the cities of Garmish and Partenkirchen.

From the summit, it is possible to see three different nations. But for skiers, the view can be brief. There are more than fifty miles (eighty kilometers) of trails on Zugspitze, all leading down.

THE RHINE VALLEY

From its source in southern Switzerland, the Rhine River passes through most of western Germany, eventually emptying into the North Sea in the Netherlands. Through mountain canyons and broad valleys, the Rhine winds its way for some 820 miles (1,320 kilometers) from its source to the sea. It also seems to wind its way through the soul of Germany.

Long ago, German noblemen built great castles on high hills

and cliffs overlooking the Rhine. In the year 1254, a large group of towns situated along the river joined together to form the Rhine League. The alliance was an important milestone in the eventual formation of a German nation. Along the Rhine's often hilly and forested banks, peasants and nobility alike told each other folktales for centuries. In the 1800s, the Brothers Grimm made the strange stories famous throughout the world. Many of the well-known fables in *Grimm's Fairy Tales* were born long ago along the banks of the Rhine.

Another group of old German myths, called the *Nibelungen,* tells about a cursed treasure of gold that was buried in the Rhine River. Parts of this old tale were made famous by the German opera composer Richard Wagner in the mid-1800s.

The Rhine River means far more to Germans than a source of old myths and fairy tales. Today, great barges carry hundreds of millions of tons of grain, coal, iron ore, fuel oil, wood, and other materials each year along the river. About three-quarters of all Germany's waterways freight is carried on the Rhine.

The beauty of many parts of the Rhine also makes it popular among foreign tourists and vacationing Germans. Luxurious cruise ships, some made to look like compact ocean liners, sail up and down the river. Passengers can see some of the loveliest castles, churches, villages, and forested hills in all of Europe.

During the twentieth century, the Rhine River, like many other rivers throughout Europe and the world, became dangerously polluted. The contamination of the Rhine seemed to reach its peak during the late 1970s. Since then, the quality of the water has been gradually improving. Laws passed in West Germany during the late 1980s made it virtually illegal, by the year 1990, to discharge

Pfalz Castle, on an island in the Rhine, was once a customs post.

any untreated pollutants into the Rhine. Nevertheless, the struggle to protect the Rhine River and other natural resources continues.

CLIMATE

Germany is situated in the world's temperate zone, where temperatures change moderately from season to season. Weather in the western part of the country is influenced by the Atlantic Ocean. The ocean tends to warm the air in winter and cool it in summer. The eastern part of the nation has a more continental climate with hot summers and cold winters.

In the northwestern part of the nation, the average annual temperature is about fifty degrees Fahrenheit (ten degrees Celsius). To the south, the temperature is warmer by about three degrees Fahrenheit (one and a half degrees Celsius). Rainfall is also influenced by moist air from the Atlantic Ocean. Therefore, western Germany generally receives a bit more rain than eastern Germany.

THE FEDERAL STATES

Like many other nations, Germany is divided into smaller political states, called *Länder* in the German language. There are a total of sixteen different Länder, but the three smallest—Berlin, Hamburg, and Bremen—are really city-states. They are not much larger than the metropolitan areas of the three large cities for which they are named.

When the German nation was reunited on October 3, 1990, five states, all formerly in East German territory, were added to the Federal Republic of Germany. They are named Thuringia, Saxony, Saxony-Anhalt, Brandenburg, and Mecklenburg-Vorpommern. These states are not new political divisions. All five existed earlier in the twentieth century, as late as 1952. In that year, the East German Communist government replaced them with fifteen administrative districts.

The remaining states are all in territory that was part of the Federal Republic (West Germany) following World War II. They are Baden-Württemberg, Bavaria, Saarland, Rhineland Palatinate, Hesse, North Rhine-Westphalia, Lower Saxony, and Schleswig-Holstein.

Some German Länder are as well known throughout the world as some small nations. Germany's largest state, Bavaria, is located in the southeastern corner of the country. The southern portion of the state is a famous vacationland, noted for Alpine mountains and scenic lakes located between Alpine foothills.

Erecting the Berlin Wall in 1961

Three German states are named wholly or in part after Saxony, one of the most famous areas of Europe. At various times in history, including the early years of the twentieth century, Saxony was an independent kingdom. More than a thousand years earlier, it was the home of a Germanic tribe called the Saxons. The Saxons were fierce warriors who had a tremendous impact on European history.

The city-state of Berlin has played a pivotal role in modern history. The city itself was largely destroyed during World War II. It was gradually rebuilt in the decade that followed. For twenty-eight years—during the Cold War—Berlin was a divided city. A huge division, the Berlin Wall, was built to keep people living in Communist East Berlin from traveling to democratic West Berlin. Then in 1989, after the Cold War ended, the crumbling Communist government of East Germany opened gates in the wall. A flood of East Germans crossed to the West. Some brought sledge hammers to attack the hated symbol of Communist failure. The German nation was fully reunited in less than a year.

Chapter 3

EARLY HISTORY

In 1856 a skeleton was found buried in Germany's Neanderthal ravine, part of the enormous Neander Valley near the city of Düsseldorf on the Rhine River. The skeleton appeared much like the bones of a modern human being, but seemed to be very old.

Eventually, scientists decided that this Neanderthal man, named after the German valley, was a direct relative of modern human beings. Neanderthals lived on the northern plains of Germany, and many other places in Europe, the Middle East, and Africa, as much as a hundred thousand years ago. The ancient Neanderthals hunted mammals and other animals that lived around the edges of huge Ice Age glaciers that still covered much of the land.

Visitors to modern Germany can still see the ancient bones discovered in 1856. They are on display at the *Rheinisches Landesmuseum* ("Rhineland Museum") in the city of Bonn.

ANCIENT GERMANIC TRIBES

The first groups of modern human beings known to have inhabited today's Germany were Celts. By the fifth century B.C.,

Celtic people were the most powerful force in Europe. They spread over much of the continent, plundering Rome in 390 B.C. The vast empire of the Celts spread from England in the west to Turkey in the east.

By early standards, the Celts were highly civilized people. The various tribes shared a common oral language. Pottery, jewelry, and bronze weapons were skillfully decorated. They also shared a well-developed system of religion and social customs. Nevertheless, their centralized government, if one existed at all, was not well organized.

The military successes of the Celts eventually led to their downfall. By the second century B.C., they had expanded over so much of Europe that they were vulnerable to invasion in the heart of their empire. Attacking them from the north and east, a large group of tribes called the *Teutons* gradually took over their land in present-day Germany. Over the next few centuries, the Celts were absorbed into other cultures. Even today, however, in some remote areas of the British Isles, strong echoes of the ancient Celtic language can still be heard in conversations.

Neanderthal and Celtic people may have been the first to live in Germany, but the Teutons gave the country its real character. Today, the phrases "Teutonic tribes" and "Germanic tribes" are used interchangeably to describe the same early people.

THE TEUTONIC TRIBES OF GERMANY

More than two thousand years ago, Roman soldiers fought for control of a part of Europe they called Gaul. Ancient Gaul included all of present-day France and parts of other nations as well, including the small area of Germany west of the Rhine River.

Hermann's triumph over the Romans

By the year 50 B.C. the Roman general Julius Caesar had conquered most of Gaul. For a time, the Rhine Valley fell under the control of Roman soldiers. But the Teutonic tribes living near the river soon rebelled against Roman taxes.

In the year A.D. 9, the Teutonic soldier Hermann (called Arminius in Latin) defeated a huge Roman army of about twenty thousand soldiers in the dense Teutoburg Forest. The Battle of Teutoburg Forest was one of the most important events in ancient European history. Partly because of it, the major language groups of Europe were divided roughly at the Rhine River. To the west of it, the people conquered by the Romans developed Roman customs and Romance languages. To the east of the Rhine, people kept their Teutonic languages and customs. The effects of that two-thousand-year-old battle can clearly be felt by people traveling across Europe today.

Many Germans regard Hermann as their first national hero. Two of his favorite sayings are remembered to this day: "In unity there is strength!" and "Rather death than slavery!"

In the year A.D. 98, the Roman historian Tacitus published a book called *On the Origin, Location, Manners, and Inhabitants of Germany*, better known as *The Germania*. In it, he wrote: "I agree with those who think that the tribes of Germany are free from all trace of intermarriage with foreign nations, and that they appear as a distinct, unmixed race, like none but themselves. Hence it is, that the same physical features are to be observed throughout so vast a population. All have fierce blue eyes, reddish hair, and huge bodies fit only for sudden exertion . . . .

"Iron is not plentiful among them," Tacitus continued, "as may be inferred from the nature of their weapons. Only a few make use of swords or long lances. Ordinarily they carry a spear . . . .

"It is a well-known fact that the people of Germany have no cities, and that they do not even allow buildings to be erected close together. They live scattered about, wherever a spring, or a meadow, or a wood has attracted them."

THE CHANGING FACE OF EUROPE

During the first few centuries A.D., the Teutonic tribes of Germany began to change. A number of the smaller, older tribes joined together, sometimes with wandering tribes from other parts of Europe, and became larger and more powerful. Among the stronger new tribes were the Alemanni, Bavarians, Burgundians, Franks, Goths, Saxons, Thuringians, and Vandals. Some of these tribes crossed the Rhine River to battle Roman soldiers still in control to the west. Other European and Asian

Clovis defeats the Goths; Roman aqueduct and bath ruins in Trier (right inset)

tribes also battled Roman soldiers. Throughout Europe, Roman soldiers and politicians became less powerful.

Of the many Teutonic tribes that battled for control of territory in central Europe, the eventual clear winners were the Franks. Clovis I, an early Frankish leader, ruled all of France and Holland and much of Germany from A.D. 481 to 511. He lived, however, not in Germany but in Paris, France. For nearly two centuries, the heirs of Clovis continued to rule much of Germany, as well as other parts of Europe.

The Frankish tribe was the most powerful in Germany, but there were many other tribes active there as well. Not all of the people living in Germany were even Teutonic. Early Frankish laws, probably written during the reign of Clovis I, reflected the area's diversity. Under those laws, for example, the fine for killing a free Frank was twice as high as the fine for killing a Roman. (On

Emperor Charlemagne ruled the Christian Western world for over thirty years.

the other hand, if a murderer killed a Frank and then placed the body in a well, or under water, or tried to hide it by covering it with branches, the fine was four times higher. Fines were paid not to the king's government, but to the victim's relatives!)

CHARLEMAGNE

During the seventh and eighth centuries, control of France and Germany was taken away from the heirs of Clovis I by a new royal family. By far the most powerful of the new leaders was named Charlemagne (Karl der Grosse in German). Raised in the Christian faith since his birth in 742, Charlemagne eventually became the ruler of most of Europe, including Germany.

Between the years 771 and 814, Charlemagne was the sole ruler of the Franks. Through diplomacy and warfare with neighboring people, he extended his control to most of the land bordered by the Atlantic Ocean and the North, Baltic, Black, and

Entrance to Aachen Cathedral

Mediterranean seas. A devout Christian, Charlemagne spent much of his energy battling the Saxons, a powerful tribe that refused to accept the Christian religion. During his reign, most of the old Teutonic tribes, including the Saxons, came under his Christian rule.

In the later years of his life, Charlemagne set up his court in the German city soon called Aix-la-Chapelle. Today named Aachen, it is the same town in which his father, Pippin, had lived. Modern visitors to Aachen can enter the *Dom*, a cathedral that Charlemagne started and which was completed a thousand years later. Inside the old church is the worn but still impressive marble throne Charlemagne used twelve hundred years ago.

In the year 800, Charlemagne led an army to Rome, where Pope Leo III had been wounded and driven from office the previous year. The Frankish king helped Leo return to power. On Christmas Day in the year 800, Charlemagne was in St. Peter's church in Rome. While he was praying at the altar, Pope Leo unexpectedly approached and proclaimed him "Emperor of the Romans." The new title revived the old idea of a Roman emperor in control of most of Western Europe.

According to a ninth-century historian, Charlemagne graciously accepted his new title but was secretly annoyed by it. A great many local rulers, especially in Italy, resented Charlemagne's new fame. The new emperor had to spend much of his time being polite to others who felt his title was improper. The struggle by Germanic kings to become "Emperor of the Romans," and soon "Holy Roman Emperor," played an important role in European history for centuries following his death.

Charlemagne died in 814 and was buried in the cathedral at Aachen. His remains are still there today. Many of the cultural and social roots of modern Germany, as well as its neighbors, can be traced to this powerful ruler. It was during his time, for example, that the word *deutsch* seems to have first appeared to describe a German language. At the time, however, Germans hardly spoke with one voice. The Teutonic tribes united by Charlemagne spoke many different dialects. Many educated Europeans, including some Frankish leaders, considered the German languages barbaric. Latin, and even a corrupted Latin that became the French language, were often more acceptable.

CONFLICT AND CONFUSION

The heirs of Charlemagne were not able to hold his empire together for long. In 843, three of his grandsons met and signed the Treaty of Verdun. That agreement divided what was left of Charlemagne's empire into three sections. One grandson, Charles the Bald, took control of the western part of the empire, roughly the area that is now France. Another grandson, Louis, took the eastern part of Charlemagne's territory, which included much of modern-day Germany. The area between the two lands was controlled by the third grandson, Lothair.

Lothair's territory, sometimes called the middle kingdom, was short-lived. Treaties signed in 870 and 880 broke it up. A portion of it went to the eastern (Germanic) empire. From this time onward, Germany's western boundary was more or less fixed around the Rhine River. The eastern boundary, however, shifted dramatically over the centuries. That eastern boundary, in fact, was the subject of heated debate between Germans and Poles as recently as the year 1990!

More than a thousand years earlier, in 911, the last of Charlemagne's heirs died. At that time, landowning noblemen and religious leaders elected a Frankish duke, Conrad I, as the new king. Many historians regard Conrad as Germany's first true king. In those days, however, he was called "King of the Franks." In the eleventh century, the kingdom was named the Roman Empire; in the thirteenth century, the Holy Roman Empire, and in the fifteenth century, the Holy Roman Empire of the German Nation.

Conrad I may have been the first king of Germany, but he hardly ruled over a true nation. Medieval Germany had no capital. Its elected king moved about regularly. He could collect taxes only from people living on land that he himself owned. Some noblemen barely recognized the king's authority.

Two kings who followed Conrad were able to command more respect from their fellow Germans. Henry I of Saxony ruled from 919 to 936; his son, Otto I (also called Otto the Great) from 936 to 973. These kings, especially Otto, had the military skill and the

Ring seal of Otto I; at that time he spelled his name Oddo.

ability to develop allies among German noblemen to make themselves very powerful. During his reign, Otto was involved in a number of bloody battles to preserve and increase his power.

In 962, Otto was crowned Holy Roman Emperor by twenty-four-year-old Pope John XII. The title undoubtedly pleased Otto, but it was hardly helpful in establishing Germany as a nation. Otto, and other Holy Roman Emperors who followed him, spent much of their time trying to control northern Italy. For centuries, German kings fretted over their "Italian policies."

At the same time, Otto followed a policy that gave certain German towns and villages, all headed by noblemen or church leaders, many of the powers of modern nations. In 965, for example, Otto issued a charter to the archbishop of Hamburg. The charter gave the archbishop the right to establish and control a market in a place called Bremen. (Today, the city of Bremen has more than a half million inhabitants.) The archbishop could administer most of the laws in his marketplace, collect taxes, and even mint money. While kings and queens in other developing European nations tried to increase their control over their subjects, German kings gave much of it away.

Over the next several hundred years, German kings fought with their own families, their neighbors, popes, residents of Italian city-states, and many others. But try as they might, the Holy Roman emperors, as the German kings were called, could not control local states and cities arising throughout Germany.

Germany was not ready to become a nation. But the growing strength of the German people would soon be felt throughout Europe.

Chapter 4

THE RISE OF GERMAN CULTURE

For a period of nearly a thousand years, from 962 to 1806, Germany was ruled by a long list of "Roman emperors" and "Holy Roman emperors." But despite the lofty titles, German emperors were hardly even true kings in their own land. They were elected by a few noblemen and church officials. In order to win votes, German kings had to sign agreements handing over much of their power to those about to elect them.

Of Germany's early rulers, one of the better known was Frederick I, also known as Frederick Barbarossa, who came to power in 1152. Frederick was the first emperor in a line of German kings, called the Hohenstaufen Dynasty, that lasted a century.

In 1273, following a period of civil war, Rudolf I was crowned emperor. Rudolf was a member of a large and wealthy family called the Hapsburgs. For the next five centuries, all but a few of Germany's emperors were members of the Hapsburg family. At various times, Hapsburgs also ruled in Austria, Bohemia, Hungary, Spain, and elsewhere. But in Germany, at least in the

The walled town of Nördlingen is an example of the past when cities were built with thick, stone walls for protection.

German states outside of present-day Austria, their power was limited. In much of Germany, real political strength was held by local princes and by officials of the Roman Catholic church. Eventually, the Hapsburgs controlled only Austria.

The kings of Germany were nearly powerless to unite the nation, but a sense of nationality began to arise anyway. The German language was becoming increasingly well developed. During the Middle Ages, two epic German poems were written that eventually achieved world-wide fame. *Parsival*, by Wolfram von Eschenbach, told the story of a man who searched for the Holy Grail of Jesus and found wisdom along the way. Gottfried von Strassburg's *Tristan und Isolde* became one of the world's most lasting love stories.

TWO GERMAN LEAGUES

During the civil wars of the mid-1200s, travel between German towns was dangerous. People who ventured out from behind walled cities and castles were endangered not only by armies at war, but by highway robbers as well. Most store owners, traders,

Walking through the gate of another fortified medieval town— Rothenberg, o.d. Tauber

and craftsmen huddled inside the thick stone walls that protected their communities. Without a king able to enforce the laws, German townspeople eventually took matters into their own hands.

In 1254, representatives of the clergy, lawyers, judges, and other leading citizens of a number of cities along the Rhine River signed a document creating the Rhine League. The league declared a general peace in the valley for a period of ten years. It also called for each member city and nobleman to appoint "four reliable men and give them full authority to settle all differences of opinion in a friendly way."

Another German league, actually founded thirteen years earlier, started slowly but soon influenced much of Europe. In 1241, representatives from a number of north German towns, including Bremen, Hamburg, Cologne, and Lübeck, created the Hanseatic League. It was established to protect residents of member towns from pirates at sea and robbers on land.

As the years passed, the Hanseatic League became a virtual nation. It set up legislatures, courts, a treasury, and established banks and offices as far away as London.

By the mid-1400s, the Hanseatic League was in decline. The number of herring in the Baltic Sea decreased. Herring was a major source of income for the north German towns. More important, the French monopolized the salt trade. Without salt, herring spoiled quickly. Nevertheless, the old Hanseatic League had tremendous importance in helping a number of German cities grow. Some of the workers in cities such as Bremen and Cologne became quite wealthy, as rich as some of the lords and ladies of the nobility. The league brought a great sense of pride to many northern German towns. Because they were not owned by a local prince, some were called "free cities." To this day, the German city-states of Bremen, Hamburg, and Lübeck refer to themselves as "Hanseatic cities."

THE GUTENBERG BIBLE

Until the mid-1450s, almost all books were copied by hand. They were, therefore, rare and expensive. Chinese printers experimented with a new type of mechanical printing, but they soon abandoned it, mostly because of the complexity of their written language. A German goldsmith and printer named Johannes Gutenberg is believed to be the man who made it possible to print books relatively inexpensively for the first time.

Working in a shop in Mainz, Gutenberg cast metal squares, each with a letter of the Latin alphabet raised from the otherwise flat surface of the metal piece. Several thousand of the metal pieces were then put in a special tray. Because they were made so

A page from the Gutenberg Bible

precisely, the bits of metal could be held together simply by applying pressure from the edges. When finished, the frame held all the letters that made up all the words on a page. With this hard work completed, whole pages of written words could be printed much faster than ever before.

Ink was carefully applied to just the raised letters on each piece of metal. In a large wooden press, smooth animal skin or early paper was pressed against the inked frame. When the paper was removed, another page could be printed quickly. When all the needed copies of the same page had been printed, the metal letters could be rearranged to make a new page. For the first time, it was no longer necessary to write all the words in every copy of a book by hand.

Gutenberg (right) examines a page printed with movable type.

The first copies of Gutenberg's book, a Latin version of the Christian Bible, were sold on or before August 1456. At least forty-seven copies still exist. Other Germans may have produced parts of the Bible named after Gutenberg. He had been forced to sell his press in November 1455, a few months before the earliest editions of his Bible were known to have been sold.

Gutenberg's invention, usually called movable type, soon changed Germany and the world. It helped to bring about one of the most important movements in Germany and world history: the Protestant Reformation.

MARTIN LUTHER AND THE REFORMATION

On October 31, 1517, a German monk named Martin Luther nailed a list of ninety-five statements, called *theses*, to the door of the cathedral in Wittenberg. Some of Luther's statements were complex. In general, however, he objected to a specific practice of the Roman Catholic church. Many church officials were willing to tell people that God would forgive their sins if the sinners gave

39

money to the church. Luther felt that no person had the right to sell God's thoughts.

Martin Luther was soon excommunicated (thrown out of the Catholic church) by Pope Leo X. The Holy Roman Emperor, Charles V, declared Martin Luther an outlaw. Luther probably would have been burned at the stake, but he was saved by Frederick the Wise, a German nobleman from Saxony. Frederick was one of the powerful local princes of Germany who had the right to vote for the Holy Roman Emperor. Frederick was powerful enough to save Martin Luther's life.

For a period of eleven weeks while under Frederick's protection in the Wartburg castle, Luther translated the New Testament of the Bible from Greek to German. His translation was soon printed and made widely available. All at once, many competing forms of the German language became one—the language of Martin Luther's Bible.

Luther believed that the world was about to end. He called the printing press "God's last and greatest gift." He used it like no one else before him and few who followed. From his home town of Wittenberg, he wrote essay after essay, many criticizing the Roman Catholic church. By 1523, his articles had been printed 1,300 times. Perhaps a million copies of his writings were circulating around Germany. Before his death from natural causes in 1546, Luther had written enough to fill up 102 enormous books. All were printed on the movable-type press.

Although his writings were sometimes hard to understand, Luther's basic message was clear. True Christians, he felt, should obey the word of God, not necessarily the rules of Catholic clergymen who claimed to speak for God. Through Bible study and prayer, Christians could learn how God expected them to

Martin Luther (above);
Luther nails his theses to the door
of the Wittenberg Cathedral (left)

behave. All too often, Luther believed, the Catholic church stood in the way of God and His people. Today's Lutheran church is based on many of the teachings of Martin Luther. All Protestant churches are an outgrowth of the religious revolution he started. Tragically, that revolution brought Germany into more than a century of brutal religious warfare.

THE THIRTY YEARS' WAR

For decades, Protestant Germans battled Catholic Germans over religion, property, money, and political power. An agreement signed in 1555, called the Peace of Augsburg, failed to keep the peace for long. The ruling Hapsburg kings remained Roman Catholic. Whenever possible, the Catholics battled Protestants and destroyed Protestant churches. The Protestants fought back.

Starting in 1618, much of Europe was drawn into the conflict. In what became known as the Thirty Years' War, soldiers from England, France, Denmark, and Sweden helped German

Protestant states battle the Catholic armies of the Holy Roman Empire. Most of the battles were fought on German soil. During the Thirty Years' War, at least half of Germany's people died in battle or from diseases and famines caused by war.

The war ended in 1648 with the Treaty of Westphalia. Some German states were given to France and Sweden. Switzerland and the Netherlands, once considered part of the Holy Roman Empire, were officially removed from it. Austria ended many of its ties with the remaining German states and became increasingly independent. Religion never again played an important role in German politics.

GERMAN STATES IN TRANSITION

Beginning in the eighteenth century an area in northeast Germany called Brandenburg, with the city of Berlin at its center, allied itself with other empires and became the most powerful of the German states. In 1657, Brandenburg's prince, Frederick William I, obtained control of another area of northeast Germany called Prussia. Brandenburg-Prussia became an independent kingdom—called Prussia—in 1701.

Large parts of the seventeenth and eighteenth centuries are sometimes called the Age of Absolutism in Germany. Germany was still a crazy quilt of more than a thousand different states. Most states were ruled by a nobleman with absolute power over his subjects. Some were enlightened rulers who encouraged the arts, literature, and music. A number of large states, including Bavaria, Saxony, Brandenburg, and Hannover, became quite wealthy and powerful. Nevertheless, little sense of democracy or self-government developed in the area.

*Frederick the Great,
king of Prussia*

There were a few exceptions. Free city-states such as Hamburg and Bremen, members of the old Hanseatic League, were more or less self-governed throughout the Age of Absolutism.

In 1740, Frederick II, better known as Frederick the Great, began his forty-six-year reign in Prussia. He lost little time trying to add to his greatness. The same year he took the throne, Frederick sent armies to attack Hapsburg land in present-day Poland. For portions of the next 126 years, the kings of Prussia fought with the Hapsburgs of Austria for control of the German states between them. During much of that time, Prussia held the upper hand.

Early in the nineteenth century, Prussia and Austria put aside their differences long enough to fight together against France.

A SPREADING REVOLUTION IN FRANCE

In 1789, the people of France began a rebellion against the French king and other members of the aristocracy. The princes of Germany, as well as the Holy Roman emperor, viewed the French revolutionaries as a threat to government everywhere. The princes were as interested in maintaining their power as they were in assuring "good" government. The worst fears of the Germans soon came true.

In 1805, the self-proclaimed emperor of France, Napoleon Bonaparte, attacked and occupied more than three hundred states in central and southern Germany. The following year, Napoleon forced Emperor Francis II of Austria to give up the ancient title of Holy Roman emperor. In October 1806, Napoleon's armies invaded Prussia. Only the help of Russian soldiers saved Prussia from total destruction. Finally, in the year 1813, Prussian soldiers defeated Napoleon's army around the city of Leipzig. The French emperor's dream of a vast empire ended two years later. His armies were crushed by British and Prussian forces in present-day Belgium.

When Napoleon was defeated, the Congress of Vienna rearranged many of the nations of Europe. According to the terms of the Congress, the number of German states was reduced from more than three hundred to thirty-nine. Prussian territory was vastly increased. An assembly of all the states, called the *Bundestag*, was set up in Frankfurt. The German states who sent representatives to the assembly, while supposedly independent, were largely controlled by Prussia and Austria.

A GOLDEN AGE OF LITERATURE AND MUSIC

In the years before, during, and after the French Revolution, German artists raised music and literature to new heights. The Austrians Franz Joseph Haydn and Wolfgang Amadeus Mozart perfected a form of orchestral music called the symphony. The greatest of all composers of symphonies, Ludwig van Beethoven,

Beethoven's birthplace in Bonn

was born in Bonn, Germany, but spent much of his life in Vienna. All three of these great musicians composed many other forms of music as well. Other great German composers followed them.

Literature, too, flourished during this golden age of German culture. The German language, once considered barbaric, was enriched by poets and writers such as Johann Wolfgang von Goethe and Friedrich Schiller. These great artists, and many others, helped the people of Germany develop a sense of a German nation years before one really existed.

*A portrait of Goethe (above)
and a statue of Schiller (right)*

THE RISE OF GERMAN NATIONALISM

Many different German states had worked together to defeat the armies of Napoleon. A new sense of patriotism was gathering across the land. Many Germans were beginning to feel that it was time to put aside their differences and form a nation. A new national government would help to end some of the social injustices brought about by centuries of rule by kings and princes.

In 1848 another revolution led by common citizens broke out in France. Unrest soon spread to many of the thirty-nine separate states of Germany. Alarmed by the uprising, political leaders established a German national Parliament in the city of Frankfurt on May 18, 1848. Hoping to ease the unrest of the German people, the politicians wrote a national constitution that would have granted some limited voting rights to many German citizens.

Unfortunately, the new Parliament failed the year after it was founded. The two strongest Germanic powers, Prussia and

Austria, refused to cooperate. Because common people would be allowed to share in some parts of government, Frederick William IV, king of Prussia, refused to accept the crown offered him by the doomed Parliament. Without a king to lead the government, the Parliament disbanded. Many Germans were terribly disappointed. Conditions went back to the way they had been before 1848. The thirty-nine German states were largely controlled by Prussia and Austria. Many people emigrated to other countries, in particular to the United States. Among them was a young man named Carl Schurz, who eventually became a major general in America's Union army and later a United States senator, secretary of the interior, and a leading publisher.

HAMMERING OUT A NATION

Since it had risen to power under Frederick the Great, Prussia had the most powerful armies of all the German states. In 1861, William I became the new king of Prussia. The following year, William appointed a brilliant but ruthless German prince, Otto von Bismarck, to the office of prime minister. During the next twenty-eight years, Bismarck masterminded the unification of Germany under Prussian leadership. He also helped his new country become the most powerful nation in Europe. During the same period Bismarck also crushed a democratic movement that had been growing in Prussia for decades.

He began his work by tricking Austria into joining him in a war with Denmark in 1864. Quickly, the two allies seized the Danish-controlled states of Schleswig and Holstein. Nearly as quickly, Bismarck started an argument with Austrian officials. In the Seven Weeks' War of 1866, Prussia defeated the armies of Austria. The peace treaty that ended the brief war gave Prussia four more German states as well as Schleswig and Holstein. At the same time, twenty-two German states north of the Main River were linked by the North German Confederation. Under the confederation, each state kept its own government, but the armies of all the states were commanded by the king of Prussia.

The French government worried about Prussia's growing military power and maneuvered to check it. In 1870 the Franco-Prussian tensions led to the next war. Prussia fought with France, and even states in southern Germany, not officially part of Prussia, came to Prussia's aid. France was quickly defeated and forced to give new territories to Prussia.

THE GERMAN NATION IS BORN

Prussia's military success was celebrated throughout the remaining independent German states. Germans everywhere called for a single German nation. On April 14, 1871, a new German legislature, called the *Reichstag*, approved a draft constitution for the German empire, or *Reich*.

On January 18, 1871, months before the constitution was approved, William I, King of Prussia, was named emperor, or *Kaiser*, of Germany. The real force holding the nation together, however, was Prince Otto von Bismarck. Bismarck was a brilliant leader and helped make his new nation rich and powerful. But he distrusted democracy. At a time when other nations grew increasingly democratic, Germany did not. Its lack of democratic traditions would have tragic consequences in the twentieth century.

Chapter 5

ONE GERMANY, OR TWO?

Prince Otto von Bismarck served as the unified nation's reich chancellor for nineteen years, from 1871 to 1890. Kaiser William allowed his chancellor to make many important decisions.

After unification, Germany quickly joined much of Western Europe in what is called the Industrial Revolution. During this era, huge factories began to be built in Germany. Machines, at first, were powered by steam engines. In the 1870s and the 1880s, German engineers designed the first gasoline-powered engines and the first cars to run successfully with them.

Under Bismarck, the new nation enjoyed two decades of peace with its neighbors. By carefully choosing which foreign nations to befriend, Germany was assured an important place in European political life.

Bismarck's foreign policies were wise, but his tactics at home were disastrous. The Industrial Revolution demanded workers to run the new factories. In some other countries, workers organized

Kaiser William I (left) and Otto von Bismarck, known as the "Iron Chancellor" (right)

trade unions to demand better wages. Bismarck, fearing the power of common Germans, virtually outlawed unions. In Germany, factory workers remained desperately poor. To maintain his power, Bismarck helped pass new laws that seemed to help ordinary people. But behind the scenes, he always sided with Germany's richest and most powerful families, sometimes at the expense of common people.

Kaiser William died of cancer in 1888. Four months before the Kaiser's death, his son became emperor. Kaiser William II, grandson of William I, became the new emperor the same year his grandfather and father died. The new kaiser was not a wise ruler. Seeing that many Germans were poor, he decided to take their minds off their poverty by trying to expand German power abroad. He fired Chancellor Bismarck in 1890 and began building a huge fleet of German warships. Many European nations were alarmed by Germany's growing military buildup.

Headlines from The New York Times *detailing Archduke Ferdinand's assassination*

In the early years of the twentieth century, Kaiser William II made speech after speech that seemed to threaten foreign nations. At home, he failed to win the loyalty of German workers. Tensions increased throughout Germany and Europe. Many Germans were allowed to vote in elections for representatives to the Reichstag. But the legislature had limited power. One political party, the Social Democrats, won millions of votes but was totally excluded from the government.

WORLD WAR I

Germany had little direct responsibility for the outbreak of World War I. However, the bombastic speeches by Kaiser William II and other German leaders, as well as the nation's military buildup, seemed to set the stage for a war. The conflict was provoked by the assassination of Francis Ferdinand, heir to the throne of

Kaiser William II (left) receded into the background at the outbreak of World War I while Paul von Hindenburg (above) exerted his will.

Austria, and his wife on June 28, 1914 in Sarajevo, Bosnia. Bosnia was an Austrian territory claimed by Serbia. To punish Serbia, Austria-Hungary declared war against Serbia on July 28, 1914. As Russia prepared to support Serbia, Germany declared war on Russia on August 1, 1914. Shortly thereafter France called up troops to support Russia, and Germany then declared war on France. Kaiser William II hoped to defeat the French army quickly and obtain some French land for Germany. Instead, his forces were defeated in the Battle of the Marne. Germany's western front with France became stalemated in trench warfare that lasted for years. During the war, German soldiers such as Field Marshal Paul von Hindenburg and General Erich Ludendorff dictated many day-to-day affairs of the country.

The United States entered the war in April 1917 and soon turned the tide against Germany and its few allies. Ludendorff continued to call for "peace through victory," while the German army and economy were destroyed. More than half of the eleven million men in Germany's armed forces were killed or wounded.

An armistice, ending World War I, was signed on November 11, 1918. But for weeks before the treaty was finalized, America and its allies had demanded a more democratic form of government in Germany. Many war-weary Germans agreed. As another price for peace, Germans had to surrender large areas of land, as well as colonies abroad, to other nations. On November 10, the day before the armistice was signed, Kaiser William II fled to the Netherlands. For the first time, the German nation seemed ready for a truly democratic form of government.

THE WEIMAR REPUBLIC

In January 1919, Germans elected representatives to a national assembly that soon met in the city of Weimar, once the home of both Goethe and Schiller. Most of the representatives were members of one of several political parties. The largest party was the Social Democratic party, once totally excluded from government under Kaiser William II. With two other parties, the German Democrats and the Catholic Center, the Social Democrats controlled the Weimar assembly.

Few of the nation's politicians had any experience with democratic governments. In 1925, Paul von Hindenburg, the former World War I field marshal, was elected president. Like so many other German politicians, Hindenburg was distrustful of democracy and did little to promote it. When the worldwide economic depression of 1929 reached Germany, unemployment soared. Germans became increasingly dissatisfied with their government. Some felt that the nation's first real experiment with democracy had failed.

HITLER'S NAZI PARTY

During the early 1930s, a small political party called the National Socialist German Workers' party grew dramatically. The leader of the Nazi party, as it was sometimes called, was Adolf Hitler. Hitler gave fiery speeches blaming Germany's economic problems on Jews, Communists, gypsies, and other groups. Tragically, many worried Germans began to believe him. By 1932, the Nazis became the nation's strongest political party. On January 30 of the following year, Hitler became chancellor of Germany.

From the moment he rose to power, Hitler encouraged the hatred of Jews, gradually taking away from them all their rights and liberties. Over the next few years, many Jewish people fled, including some of the nation's brightest artists, writers, and scientists. Among the great Jewish intellects driven from Germany during this period was the physicist Albert Einstein, who moved to America in 1933.

Paul von Hindenburg, Germany's president, died in 1934. Hitler immediately became president as well as chancellor. The presidency gave him control of the nation's armed forces. Although Germany was supposed to be a democratic republic, Hitler soon had the power of a dictator. During 1935 and 1936, he used his army to control parts of the nation lost after World War I. In 1938, Austria joined his growing empire.

There was a massive buildup of the German military. Many people found jobs making weapons and supplies for the German army. For some Germans, life seemed to be improving under the Nazis. For Jewish people and some others, conditions grew far worse.

Opposite page: Hitler and his staff command the attention of thousands at a parade. Adolf Hitler (inset) in 1938

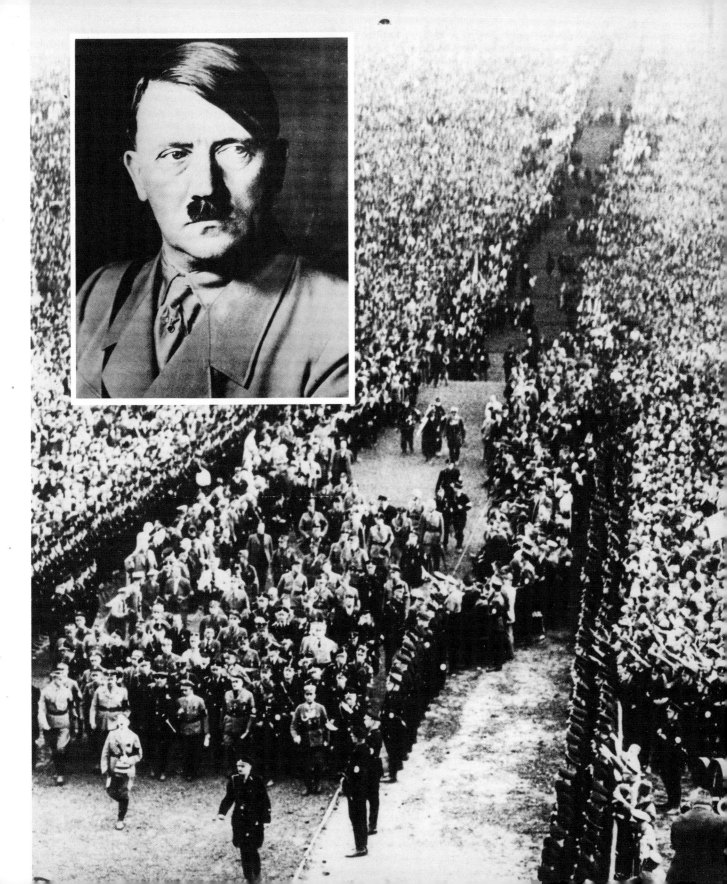

The Nazi army driving into a small Polish village (left); Buchenwald concentration camp (right)

WORLD WAR II

Hitler was not satisfied with total control of just Germany. He seemed driven to rule all of Europe. On September 1, 1939, he issued commands to invade Poland. In a series of lightning attacks, German soldiers invaded and defeated not only Poland, but Denmark, Holland, Norway, Belgium, France, Greece, and Yugoslavia as well. German soldiers also took over large areas in North Africa and marched through the western Soviet Union. Germany allied itself with Japan and, for a time, with Italy. Most other countries of the world soon opposed the three nations.

In a number of conquered European countries, the Nazis established concentration camps. There, Jews and other "enemies" of the German nation were imprisoned. By 1942, Hitler had arrived at what he called the "final solution" to the "Jewish problem." He decided to try genocide—to murder every Jewish man, woman, and child on earth. Over the next few years, about

*United States soldiers view Nazi victims (left);
American troops land in France (above)*

six million Jewish people were killed in Nazi concentration
camps. People who opposed this mad scheme were murdered as
well.

On June 6, 1944, thousands of ships carrying soldiers from the
United States, England, Canada, and other nations began landing
on the beaches of France. Soldiers from the nations allied against
Germany fought their way through Europe. Everywhere, citizens
cheered the arrival of the Allies, who freed them from the hated
grasp of German soldiers.

By the spring of 1945, Allied soldiers were marching on Berlin,
the capital of the Nazi empire. On April 30, Hitler committed
suicide. Two days later, Soviet soldiers captured Berlin. In May
1945, Germany surrendered to the United States forces in Reims,
France, and to the Soviet forces in Berlin. Japan surrendered a few
months later, ending the war.

In all of history it is difficult to find another military as ruthless
as Nazi Germany was, under Adolf Hitler's dictatorship.

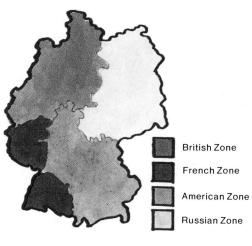

British Zone

French Zone

American Zone

Russian Zone

Badly destroyed during the war,
Berlin lost most of its historic center.

Germany in 1945

For its crimes, Nazi Germany exacted a terrible price from the nation. In addition to the millions of innocent victims who died in concentration camps, more than three million German soldiers, and an equal number of civilians, were killed during the war. A quarter of all German homes were destroyed or heavily damaged in airplane bombing raids and ground battles. Following the war, millions of German survivors tried to stay alive with very little food, clothing, or shelter.

GERMANY IS DIVIDED

As a result of the war, Germany was forced to give up some of its northern territory to the Soviet Union and Poland. The land that remained was divided into four occupied zones. Each of the most important Allied countries—the United States, England, the Soviet Union, and France—controlled one zone. The capital, Berlin, was not included in any of the four zones. It was governed by all four occupying nations.

After World War II, Berlin was divided into four zones. In 1949 the Russian Zone became East Berlin and the three other zones West Berlin.

Most of the Allied nations planned to reunify Germany within a few years. The Allies also ruled over their parts of Germany somewhat selfishly. Each of the conquering nations developed its own interests in rebuilding the defeated land. Squabbles between American and Soviet leaders grew particularly strong.

Almost immediately following the war, Soviet troops began building fortifications separating Eastern Europe, which they controlled, from the nations of Western Europe. On March 5, 1946, the English statesman Winston Churchill noted that "an Iron Curtain has descended across the continent." A portion of the Iron Curtain, 866 miles long (1,394 kilometers), cut the nation of Germany into two parts.

With unexpected swiftness, Soviet forces were in control of many Eastern European nations, including, among others, Poland, Hungary, Czechoslovakia, and a large section of northeastern Germany. The city of Berlin was not officially part of the Soviet zone, but Soviets decided to take total control of it anyway. In 1948, soldiers from the Soviet Union set up a blockade around Berlin. For nearly a year, during what was called the Berlin Air Lift, airplanes carried food and other supplies into the city. The blockade was finally lifted.

The three German zones formerly occupied by American, British, and French forces were merged to become a single independent nation on May 23, 1949. Best known as West Germany, the new sovereign state was officially called the Federal Republic of Germany (FRG). In West Germany, elections were held to select new political leaders. With the help of billions of dollars in aid, much of it from the U.S., West Germany was able to recover from the devastation of World War II. Within a few more years, the West German economy became Europe's richest. The part of Germany occupied by soldiers from the Soviet Union did not fare as well.

The former Soviet zone of Germany officially became a new country on October 7, 1949. It was named the German Democratic Republic (GDR), but was often called East Germany. Despite its name, the German Democratic Republic was not a democracy. Meaningful elections were not held in the GDR for forty-one years. In the meantime, the East German economy was directed by Communist officials. Although businesses and factories in East Germany eventually became the most productive of all the Communist Bloc nations, they trailed far behind those of West Germany.

THE TWO GERMANYS

For four decades following its creation in 1949, the economic might of West Germany grew at dizzying speed. In 1948, the United States and other countries launched the European Recovery Program, also called the Marshall Plan. To help them recover from the destruction of World War II, billions of dollars of aid and loans were made available to the nations of Western Europe, including West Germany. With the help of the Marshall Plan, West German business quickly became successful.

The people who developed the Marshall Plan originally

West Germany lay on one side of the barbed-wire fence, East Germany on the other.

intended to help the nations of Eastern Europe as well as those in the West. But the Soviet government refused to allow that aid to be extended to the nations it now controlled, including East Germany. The GDR could only turn to the Soviet Union for help. The Soviet military had suffered more than twenty million casualties in World War II, more than any other Allied nation. The government of the Soviet Union could afford little sympathy for the nation that had started the war. Instead of giving aid, the Soviets stripped East Germany of what little wealth remained.

Even by the early 1950s, it was clear that West Germans enjoyed a higher standard of living than their relatives in the GDR. In 1953, labor strikes and riots broke out in East Berlin and other GDR cities. The protest was smashed by Soviet soldiers and tanks. Many East Germans fled to the West.

In Germany and elsewhere in Europe, the Iron Curtain was made of steel, cement, and barbed-wire fences. Deadly mine fields and explosive booby traps were hidden near it. Spaced all along the wall were watchtowers housing electronic spy equipment and soldiers trained in the use of machine guns and other weapons, all readily at hand.

Markers in front of the Berlin Wall honor those who died trying to flee East Berlin.

The Iron Curtain was weakest in Berlin, the divided city within East Germany. During the 1950s, many Germans managed to escape to democratic West Berlin from Communist East Berlin. But in 1961, a second iron curtain was built, this one in the heart of Germany's largest city. Called the Berlin Wall, the huge concrete structure remained in place for nearly thirty years. Throughout almost all of that time, any East German who even came close to the wall risked being arrested or killed.

Despite the Iron Curtain and the Berlin Wall, many East Germans risked their lives by attempting to flee to the West. In 1979, two families flew over the Iron Curtain in a hot air balloon. Where the wall crossed a river, one enterprising man sailed under it in a homemade submarine. Others dug tunnels under the wall; a few flew homemade airplanes over it. Many just ran for their lives, hoping not to step on mines or be hit by machine-gun fire. Estimates of the number of people who succeeded, as well as those who were captured or killed trying, vary widely.

Former West German chancellor, Willy Brandt, delivers a speech to the united German Parliament on October 4, 1990. This banner held during the East Berlin demonstrations on October 8, 1989 reads: "Perestroika! Learning from the Soviet Union means learning to win."

Throughout most of the 1980s, the majority of East Germans were resigned to living their lives under a Communist government. Although their standard of living was low, it was higher than in all other Communist nations.

In the East there also were a few advantages. Housing, food, education, and medical care, although seldom first-rate, were guaranteed to all. In addition, few East Germans were unemployed.

During the 1970s Willy Brandt, who was mayor of West Berlin from 1957 to 1966 and chancellor of West Germany from 1969 to 1974, worked to normalize relations between East and West Germany. By the 1980s, some East Germans could travel to the West to visit family.

After 1985, when Gorbachev announced *glasnost* and *perestroika*, East Germans dreamed of greater freedoms and the higher standard of living that could be enjoyed in the West. As recently as the first half of 1989, few thought the dream could come true any time soon. But in the second half of that same year, people everywhere were shocked by the changes sweeping across eastern Europe.

THE UNIFICATION OF GERMANY

During the year 1989, widespread dissatisfaction with
Communist governments throughout Eastern Europe turned into
massive demonstrations. One by one, the governments of these
countries began to topple. In early September 1989, the
government of Hungary decided to allow unrestricted travel to
Austria, across the Iron Curtain. More than fifty thousand East
Germans moved to West Germany via Hungary and Austria.

In a state of shock, East German government officials celebrated
the fortieth birthday of the GDR on October 7, 1989. That day,
demonstrations against the government were held throughout the
land. Larger protests followed, including a gathering of nearly a
million dissatisfied Germans in East Berlin on November 4.

On November 7, many members of the government of East
Germany were forced to resign. Two days later, the Berlin Wall
was opened. In front of thousands of cheering people and a
throng of television and newspaper reporters, Germans began
tearing down the wall. Within a matter of months, the wall had
almost completely disappeared.

Communist officials hoped that opening the Iron Curtain would
encourage East Germans to stay at home. It did not. In November
alone, 133,429 East Germans moved to West Germany. The total
for the year, to that point, was nearly a third of a million. During
the same period, world leaders, including Chancellor Helmut
Kohl of West Germany, President George Bush of the United
States, and President Mikhail Gorbachev of the Soviet Union,
began discussing the possibility of uniting the two Germanys.

There were a number of serious problems. East German money
was virtually worthless outside of Communist nations. A unified

Both East and West Berliners attacked the wall on the eve of unification.

nation could have only one type of currency. What would happen to the savings of East Germans? Another problem involved military defense. The nations of Western Europe, including West Germany, belonged to NATO, the North Atlantic Treaty Organization. Eastern European countries, including East Germany, belonged to the Warsaw Pact, dominated by the Soviet Union. To which military alliance would a unified Germany belong? Finally, East Germans and Poles had been arguing for decades about the location of the border between them. The border dispute threatened German unification.

Solutions to all the problems were reached in 1990. On Sunday, July 1, 1990, the economies of East and West Germany were officially merged. By terms of the treaty, East Germans would be allowed to exchange much of their nearly worthless money for

Outside Berlin's Reichstag building on October 3, 1990

West German currency with the same face value. The exchange
cost the West German government a fortune.

A few days later, the Polish government gave up its insistence
on a written treaty to establish the border between Poland and the
new Germany. The existing border was allowed to continue.
Within a few more days, Soviet President Gorbachev agreed to
allow the new Germany to become a member of NATO, without a
matching membership in the Warsaw Pact. For this favor,
Germany promised approximately three billion dollars in foreign
aid to the Soviet Union.

On September 12, 1990, the Parliaments of both East and West
Germany ratified a final treaty calling for German unification on
October 3, 1990. When the day finally arrived, millions of
Germans were exhausted. They had stayed up to celebrate the
arrival of their new nation at the stroke of midnight.

GERMANY TODAY

On October 3, 1990, the German Democratic Republic (East Germany) ceased to exist. Its people became citizens of the Federal Republic of Germany (formerly West Germany). The West German flag, national anthem, and constitution now serve the people of both former states. Although it would take years to move government offices, the once-divided city of Berlin was named the capital of the new Germany. Helmut Kohl became the united nation's first chancellor, and Richard von Weizsäcker its first president.

By the early months of 1991, it was clear that German unification had created some problems. Many former East German companies, once directed by Communist bureaucrats, found it difficult to compete with more efficient companies to the west. Tens of thousands of workers from the shipbuilding and metalworking industries gathered in mass protests for more jobs and better pay. In February, the German Institute for Economic Research estimated that about 21 percent of potential workers in former East German territory were without full-time jobs. To help pay the costs of unemployment, the German government announced that it was forced to raise taxes.

Obviously, it would take years to overcome the difficulties caused by decades of political division in Germany. Some of the problems were humorous. In 1991, a phone call between the German towns of Neustadt and Sonneberg, just over two miles (four kilometers) apart, cost more than a phone call to Madrid, Spain. The two towns were once divided by the Iron Curtain, and German phone companies had not yet caught up with the times.

Hundreds of people gather at the Berlin Wall in front of the Brandenburg Gate to see if East German troops will smash through the wall at that very symbolic point (above). An organ grinder (right) entertains as Berliners cross through the Brandenburg Gate after the wall was opened.

Hamburg

Berlin ★

Leipzig

Cologne
Bonn
Dresden

Koblenz Frankfurt
Worms
Mannheim

Baden-Baden Munich

Chapter 6

SNAPSHOTS
OF A VARIED LAND

The largest city in Germany, and its official capital, is Berlin. In recent years, this city of more than three million inhabitants has made its share of newspaper headlines.

On November 9, 1989, people throughout the world saw televised pictures of joyous Berliners gathered around the infamous Berlin Wall. Some were climbing to the top of it; others were attacking the cement structure with sledge hammers. Much of the celebrating took place at the famous Brandenburg Gate, near the heart of Berlin. *Brandenburger Tor*, as the gate is called in German, had been built exactly two centuries earlier for Frederick William II, a Prussian king. For nearly three decades, it stood just west of the Berlin Wall.

Many parts of the wall were gone by July 2, 1990, when the subway system between East and West Berlin was relinked for the first time since 1961, the year the wall was built. On October 3, 1990, Berlin was officially unified, along with the rest of the German nation. Today, Berlin is both a city and a German federal state. It is surrounded entirely by the state of Brandenburg.

Berlin's decades of division after World War II reflect its early history as two separate villages. More than 750 years ago, there

In Berlin, the bomb-damaged Kaiser Wilhelm Remembrance Church has been kept as a memorial of World War II, and new buildings have been constructed.

Boating on the Spree River and the zoo entrance at the Tiergarten

was a little settlement called Kölln on an island in the Spree River, today called Museum Island. Nearby on the mainland, another settlement was called Berlin. The two towns began to merge in the fourteenth century.

Berlin served as the capital of Prussia in the nineteenth century and of the German nation from its birth in 1871 until the end of World War II, when the city was in total ruins. Since that time, Berlin has been rebuilt. Some buildings that look very old actually have been reconstructed to appear that way. From 1949 to 1990, the northeast portion of the city, called East Berlin, served as the capital of East Germany. Today, Berlin is once again the capital of a united Germany. Moving government offices from Bonn (West Germany's capital) to Berlin has been a gradual process.

BERLIN TODAY

Near the center of Berlin, just south of the Spree River, is a large park called the *Tiergarten* ("animal garden"). As the name suggests,

71

*The Tiergarten, founded in 1789, hosts
performing walruses and floral
displays; the facade (top left) from
a Greek Temple at Pergamon Museum*

the park contains a zoo, Germany's oldest, which was completely
rebuilt after World War II. The Tiergarten also contains lengthy
hiking trails and a number of small lakes. Most of the trees in the
park were planted since 1949. Immediately after World War II, the
existing trees were cut down by Germans desperate for firewood.

At the eastern end of the park is the famous Brandenburg Gate.
By traveling through it and heading east on the boulevard called
Unter den Linden, "Under the Linden Trees," visitors immediately
reach the historic center of Berlin. The street passes by a number
of important museums, concert halls, and other buildings before
crossing Museum Island, one of Berlin's two birthplaces. The
Pergamon Museum on Museum Island has some of the world's
most important archaeological exhibits, including a Greek temple
more than two thousand years old. The newest museum in the
area, about ten blocks south of Unter den Linden, is *Haus am*

Linden tree in bloom

Now all Berliners can enjoy a stroll along Unter den Linden Boulevard, which was formerly in East Berlin. Alexanderplatz (left)

Checkpoint Charlie, a museum remembering the Berlin Wall and its most famous crossing point, "Checkpoint Charlie."

A few blocks beyond Museum Island is *Alexanderplatz*, "Alexander Place," for years the central square of East Berlin. Today, the area is clean and modern. The dominant feature of the square is a huge television antenna tower with a revolving restaurant about halfway up. From the restaurant, it is possible to see almost all of Berlin on a clear day.

After World War II, in both the Soviet and western sections, Berlin was rebuilt. Renovation and modern and postmodern architectural innovations, especially in the 1980s, make Berlin one

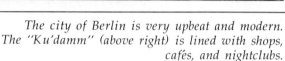

The city of Berlin is very upbeat and modern. The "Ku'damm" (above right) is lined with shops, cafés, and nightclubs.

of the more interesting cities of Europe. The city has a fast-paced spirit and a cosmopolitan lifestyle that make it an exciting place to visit. It is also one of Europe's most important industrial and business centers.

Many Berliners seeking a night out on the town flock to the street called *Kurfürstendamm*, or the "Ku'damm" for short. For decades, it was the busiest street in West Berlin. Hundreds of shops, art galleries, nightclubs, and sidewalk cafés still bring throngs of visitors to the street each year.

One of the most important groups of museums in the world is located in what used to be West Berlin. Since it is situated far from the center of the city, it is often overlooked by visitors. Nevertheless, the Dahlem Museum Complex is certainly worth visiting, with whole buildings devoted to paintings, history, photographs and drawings, and sculpture.

Charlottenburg Palace (above) and Sanssouci, Frederick the Great's summer palace (top right)

Another popular tourist attraction in the western part of the city is *Schloss Charlottenburg*, "Charlottenburg Palace." The palace was started in 1695 by Frederick I, but was greatly enlarged when Frederick the Great took up residence there. It has been carefully reconstructed following serious damage in World War II.

Just a short distance from the southwest city limits of Berlin is Potsdam. In that historic Berlin suburb, many Prussian kings and their relatives built second homes. One of the most popular tourist attractions is the summer palace of Frederick the Great. In the summer of 1945, America's Harry Truman, the Soviet Union's Joseph Stalin, and England's Winston Churchill met in Potsdam to determine how Germany would be governed during the post-World War II years.

Hamburg: Its harbor and the subway train called U Bahn (below), and a rooftop view of city streets (right)

HAMBURG: GERMANY'S SECOND CITY

Called *Hammaburg* when Emperor Charlemagne started it as a fort around A.D. 808, Hamburg is Germany's principal seaport and its second-largest city. Like Berlin, Hamburg is both a city and a German federal state. And, yes, the popular sandwich meat made of cooked ground beef was named after this famous city. Residents of Hamburg, in fact, are called Hamburgers.

Hamburg was one of the founders of the old Hanseatic League. It remains one of the most important seaports in Europe, even though it is about 65 miles (105 kilometers) from the North Sea. The wide Elbe River provides an inland highway for oceangoing ships to reach the city's huge port. About fifteen thousand ships sail into Hamburg each year. They carry cargoes that range from oil and construction materials to fresh fruits and vegetables. Because of the busy seaport, Hamburg is a magnet for international banks and business offices, foreign consulates, and trade shows.

Like Berlin, much of Hamburg was destroyed during World War II. Unlike the German capital, Hamburg was also virtually devastated by a fire a century earlier. However, it is difficult for visitors to tell that the city has been rebuilt two times. A number of ancient buildings, including the thirteenth-century *Jacobikirche*, "St. Jacob's Church," have been reconstructed to appear almost exactly as they did hundreds of years ago. A number of important museums in Hamburg also showcase the art and history of Germany and much of the world.

The city is also famous—and infamous—for a stretch of rowdy nightclubs, bars, and dance halls located along a street called the *Reeperbahn*. The area grew up as a place where sailors arriving at

An evening view of Hamburg with the Alster Lake

port could have a wild night out on the town. Some people regard it as the most sinful place in Europe.

The center of the city is dominated by a large artificial lake. It was made in the 1700s by damming the Alster River near where it flows into the Elbe. More than a thousand bridges cross the rivers, streams, and many canals that flow through the city limits of Hamburg. For this reason, it is sometimes called "Venice of the North."

The Chinese tower in Munich's Englischer Garten stands by a popular beer garden (left). A view of Munich (right)

THE ENCHANTMENT OF MUNICH

The capital of the state of Bavaria, far to the south of Hamburg and Berlin, Munich is the kind of city many people think typifies Germany best. To some visitors and vacationing Germans heading southward toward the Bavarian Alps, Munich marks the start of the nation's Alpine vacationland.

Germany's third-largest city was founded in 1158, when a

The Frauenkirche (left) was consecrated in 1494. The Glockenspiel (right) shows episodes from Munich's history.

Saxon prince destroyed a nearby village and started a new one at the present site of the city. Over the centuries, the rulers of Bavaria built a number of magnificent palaces near the heart of the city, most carefully reconstructed after World War II. Here too is where Adolf Hitler spent much of his youth, and where he unsuccessfully tried to take over the Bavarian government in the "Beer Hall Putsch" of 1923.

The center of downtown Munich is dominated by two huge squares that are not far apart. A street joining the two—lined with fountains and flowers—can be used only by pedestrians. One square, called *Marienplatz*, is the site of the city's famous town hall. It was built in the late 1800s, but it appears much older. At 11:00 o'clock every morning, and some other times in the

Marienplatz (above) is lined with flowers, and the streets are lined with people during Oktoberfest (left). Bands (upper left) provide music for dancing during the fest.

summer, a short concert on a large musical instrument, a *Glockenspiel*, is given. At the same time, mechanical figurines emerge from the town hall tower to do battle in a mock tournament. Two large and ancient churches, *Frauenkirche* and *Peterskirche*, are nearby.

Munich is also famous for a number of fine museums, concert halls, and especially for the *Residenz*, the palace of the rulers of old Bavaria. Perhaps the city is most famous of all for its *Oktoberfest*, a sixteen-day October festival devoted to eating, listening to oom-pah bands, wearing native costumes, and especially, drinking beer. With this tradition, it is hardly surprising that the University of Munich, one of Europe's finest schools, maintains a beer department.

A statue of Bach (left) commemorates the church where he worked during his latter years. Leipzig's town hall (above) is the oldest German Renaissance town hall.

LEIPZIG AND DRESDEN

For four decades, these two cities, just 60 miles (97 kilometers) apart, were the largest urban areas in Communist Germany after East Berlin. Today, both are in the federal state of Saxony.

During the eighteenth and nineteenth centuries, Leipzig was one of Germany's greatest cultural centers. The composer Johann Sebastian Bach spent his last twenty-seven years in Leipzig, where he wrote some of his most famous works. The operatic composer Richard Wagner was born and educated in Leipzig. Before being forced to flee Germany for his part in a political uprising in 1848, he also lived for a number of years in Dresden. The poets Johann Wolfgang von Goethe and Friedrich Schiller also spent brief parts of their lives in Leipzig. For centuries, Leipzig was known as a trade and publishing center. Dresden served as the capital of Saxony.

A pedestrian mall and park in Dresden

Today, following more than forty years of Communist rule, the people of both cities are still getting used to the ways of western-style democracies. Following German reunification, unemployment in both cities grew to alarming levels. Nevertheless, the people of Leipzig and Dresden have gotten used to dramatic changes before. The two cities were completely destroyed in World War II bombing raids. The East German government spent considerable effort reconstructing historic buildings in both cities. Before World War II, Dresden was considered one of the most beautiful cities in the world. Today, a bit of its architectural splendor has been restored.

CITIES OF THE RHINE VALLEY

Sightseers traveling on the Rhine River can see some of Germany's loveliest scenery as well as a few of its most important cities. Soon after the Rhine enters Germany from Switzerland, it

Gutenfels Fortress overlooks Pfalz Castle on the Rhine River.

passes by the scenic Black Forest. Flowing just to the east of the cities of Freiburg and Baden-Baden, the river soon arrives at a bustling river port named Mannheim.

Mannheim was built where the Neckar River flows into the Rhine. Started in the early 1600s, relatively late for cities in the Rhine Valley, Mannheim is unusual as German cities go because its oldest streets are laid out in a gridlike pattern.

Along the east bank of the Rhine just a short distance to the north is the ancient city of Worms. Some historians believe that the city is at least five thousand years old. When Germany was part of the Holy Roman Empire, a legislature, called a diet, met there many times. It was known—laugh if you must—as ''the Diet

Worms Cathedral (left) is one of Germany's best examples of high Romanesque style (eleventh and twelfth centuries). Frankfurt (above)

of Worms." Martin Luther appeared before the Diet of Worms in 1521 and was accused of heresy.

The next city along the Rhine is the city of Mainz, where the Main River flows into the Rhine from the east. Mainz has two claims to fame. Its huge cathedral was built nearly a thousand years ago. Parts of it were rebuilt after World War II. Mainz was also the home of Johannes Gutenberg, the world's first book printer. In the Gutenberg Museum, his ancient shop has been recreated as faithfully as possible.

Just east of Mainz, along the Main River, is the city of Frankfurt, one of Germany's most important economic and transportation centers. The frankfurter, or hot dog, was named after this city.

North from Mainz, the Rhine winds through the historic and scenic heart of western Germany. In its wide valley, the river passes vineyards, quaint villages, and old castles that seem like the settings from fairy tales.

Koblenz is the next major city along the Rhine. It is situated

The former Bundestag building (upper left) and the town hall in Bonn

where the Mosel River flows into the Rhine from the east. Koblenz was founded in 9 B.C. by the Roman general Nero Claudius Drusus Germanicus. Near the city, visitors can ride a chair lift up to Ehrenbreitstein Fortress, parts of which were built a thousand years ago. From there, it is possible to see much of Koblenz as well as other Rhineland castles.

The city of Bonn is located on the west bank of the Rhine, where the river has become truly enormous. For four decades, Bonn served as the capital of West Germany. Today, the German nation has officially named Berlin its capital. But most federal offices are still in Bonn. Among them are the presidential palace and the *Bundeshaus*, where the two houses of the German Parliament meet. Also in Bonn is the birthplace, now a museum,

Cologne Cathedral (left) took over six hundred years to complete. Düsseldorf (above) once a fishing village, is now the capital of North Rhine-Westphalia.

of Ludwig van Beethoven. Beethoven lived in the house at Bonngasse 20 from 1770 to 1787.

North of Bonn, the banks of the Rhine become crowded with cities and suburbs, often highly industrialized. The city of Cologne (*Köln* in German) is dominated by the magnificent cathedral built there over a period of six hundred years. With more than 900,000 residents, Cologne is the largest city in the Rhine Valley.

Just a short distance north along the river is the Rhine's second-largest city, Düsseldorf. Here, the Rhine River is so wide that only three bridges have been built across it.

Before it reaches the North Sea, the Rhine River passes by a number of smaller German cities and flows through the Netherlands.

Chapter 7

GOVERNMENT FOR
THE PEOPLE

In 1990, the noted German writer Christa Wolf published a novel called *Was Bleibt* ("*What Remains*"). In the book, Wolf drew on her own experiences living under the watchful eye of security police, called *Stasi*, in the German Democratic Republic (East Germany). In some of her earlier books, she had criticized some aspects of life under Communist rule. The security police considered her a possible enemy of the state.

Wolf had written *Was Bleibt* ten years earlier. She chose to publish it at a time when the Communist government of East Germany had already fallen apart. At the time the book was released, Germans were learning how widespread police surveillance had been throughout the GDR. They discovered, for example, that the GDR's ministry of state security had employed some eighty thousand full-time and several hundred thousand part-time agents whose main task was to spy on their fellow citizens.

East Berliners flash victory signs during a demonstration for reforms in 1989.

Wolf found herself in a bit of hot water following the publication of her book. Some people complained that she had not been critical enough of East Germany's Communist government while it was still in power. The timing of her book, they said, suggested cowardice.

In public appearances just before her book was published, Wolf pointed out that there were advantages to socialism. In a joint appeal with a fellow writer, Wolf called for her fellow citizens "to develop a socialist alternative to the Federal Republic [West Germany]." She also said: "It could be vital for both German states if certain traditions—revolutionary traditions . . . are preserved." Some critics complained that her remarks were standing in the way of progress toward ending Communist domination in eastern Germany.

When Communists ruled East Germany, Christa Wolf was suspected of being *against* communism. When the Communists lost power, she was accused of being *for* communism. It is hard to understand how she also could be accused of cowardice.

As a whole, the people of the new Germany were in no mood to follow Wolf's advice to slow down the unification process. With only minor changes, the government, laws, health and welfare programs, and educational systems of West Germany were extended quickly to the new states of former East Germany. Wolf's experiences show, however, that government, particularly in Germany, can be a touchy subject.

GERMANY'S BASIC LAW

The German constitution called the *Grundgestz*, or "Basic Law," was adopted in 1949, the same year that the two Germanys officially became separate states. Over the years some changes were added, but amendments to the constitution have been relatively few. On October 3, 1990, the constitution was extended, with some amendments, to the new states of former East Germany.

The first part of the constitution describes the rights of all German citizens. The drafters of the constitution remembered all too well how liberties had been trampled by National Socialism under Adolf Hitler. They wanted to make it exceptionally difficult to repeat that experience. One of the basic themes of the constitution is that the government exists for the benefit of the people, and not the other way around. The remaining parts of the constitution describe federal and local governments, public finances, and defense.

THE FEDERAL PRESIDENT

The German president, according to the constitution, is elected
by a group of people who gather specifically for that purpose in a
Federal Convention. The electors are made up of legislators from
the federal *Bundestag*, "House of Representatives" and an equal
number of representatives chosen by state legislatures. The
president serves a five-year term and can be reelected only once.

The powers of the German president are limited. Many
historians believe a powerful presidency was one of the main
reasons German democracy failed under the Weimar Republic. In
general, the president represents Germany in relations with other
nations and can hire many government workers. Under certain
circumstances, such as matters of national importance, the
president can call for early legislative elections.

THE FEDERAL LEGISLATURE

Under the terms of the German constitution, national laws are
passed by one and sometimes two legislative bodies. The
Bundestag is involved in the creation of all legislation. A second
body, the *Bundesrat*, "Federal Council," takes part in some
legislation, especially those laws that pertain to individual states.
More than half of all German legislation must be approved by
both bodies.

Members of the Bundestag are elected to four-year terms by
German citizens who cast secret ballots. In addition to passing
laws, this body elects a powerful leader, called a chancellor, who
is nominated by the federal president. The chancellor enjoys many

of the powers of a president in other nations. Members of the Bundestag also debate issues of national interest. Many meetings of the Bundestag are shown on television so that the German people can see what their representatives are doing.

Members of the second legislative body, the Bundesrat, are made up of officials from the sixteen German states. They are not directly elected by German citizens, although state governments are. Members of the Bundesrat generally must approve more than half of Germany's legislation. They also can make a formal objection to laws in which they are not directly involved. The objection can be overruled by the Bundestag.

THE FEDERAL CONSTITUTIONAL COURT

The word Germans use to describe their highest court is quite a mouthful. It's called the *Bundesverfassungsgericht*, which means, as you may have guessed, "Federal Constitutional Court." This court is responsible for making sure that all German laws and policies follow the guidelines of the Basic Law. Before 1949, there was no similar court in Germany. Some historians believe that this was another reason for the failure of the old Weimar Republic.

The Constitutional Court can declare federal, state, or local laws unconstitutional. It also will hear cases concerning private citizens who feel that their rights have not been respected by other courts. The Constitutional Court is made up of two groups of eight judges. Elected by the legislature, judges serve a twelve-year term and cannot be reelected. There are many other federal courts beneath the high court. Most judges in these other courts are appointed for life.

STATE AND LOCAL GOVERNMENTS

Some of Germany's sixteen states (Länder), and many of its cities and towns, have long histories of local government. Many have their own constitutions and traditions. Federal law gives local governments a great deal of freedom in setting their own policies. But there are two guidelines that local governments must follow. First, state governments must allow local communities to manage their own affairs, within the framework of the law. Second, all local governments must be organized by democratic principles.

In general, state governments are responsible for overseeing the activities of schools and police departments, and for enforcing federal law within their boundaries. Local governments are usually concerned with public transportation, the construction of schools, hospitals, and public buildings, control of public utilities, the maintenance of local roads, and so on. Many of the taxes needed for these projects are raised by local government as well.

German states have their own state legislatures. Most states are divided into a number of smaller counties, each with a legislature. In general, German citizens are encouraged to run their societies at the local level. When problems become too large for a local government to manage, the matter is usually taken over at a higher level of government.

POLITICAL PARTIES

Most German politicians who run in federal and state elections belong to a political party. The citizens who vote for them may

*Demonstrators in Leipzig (above), 1989;
the Green party (right) in a
peace march in Bonn, 1981*

consider themselves members of that party as well. People who
belong to the same political party usually hold similar opinions
about the problems and opportunities facing the nation. The Basic
Law recognizes the role of political parties "in the forming of the
political will of the people." According to all state and federal
election laws, a political party must get at least 5 percent of the
total vote to send representatives to the legislature.

On March 18, 1990, the people of East Germany voted in their
first free elections since Hitler became a dictator. Although
German unification was still nearly eight months away, the voters

Chancellor Kohl (left) shakes hands with Lothar de Maiziere, former East German prime minister, prior to the unification party.

understood that they were helping to shape a new Germany. More than 93 percent of the area's eligible voters cast ballots for their new state representatives.

The results gave a big victory to the Christian Democratic Union of West German Chancellor Helmut Kohl, which won more than 40 percent of the total vote. Another West German party, called the Social Democratic party, won about 22 percent of the vote. The party of Democratic Socialism, the Communist party which previously controlled East Germany, managed to get only 16 percent of the total. In resounding fashion, the people of East Germany rejected the policies of their Communist government.

German teenagers' tastes in dress,
social activities, and music are very
similar to other teenagers in
industrialized countries.

Chapter 8

LEARNING AND
WORKING

The German nation is a rich mixture of diverse regions. Most have centuries-old traditions that make them surprisingly different from their neighbors. Add to that the years Germany was a divided nation, as well as its emphasis on state governments, and it is clear that working and learning in today's Germany varies a great deal from place to place.

By law, all German children must attend school from the age of six to sixteen. During their final school years, however, some students may attend vocational school part-time. Rules vary from state to state. According to the German constitution, all students must receive religious training until the age of fourteen. Older students can decide whether to continue their spiritual instruction. Most decide not to. Free public schools are available to all German children. Some students go to private schools, which charge tuition.

Almost all German students get a summer vacation that lasts six weeks or so. During summer recess, many states and cities offer special holiday passes and other programs that let groups of students take organized field trips inexpensively.

Students practicing at a music school

KINDERGARTEN

Kindergarten is a German tradition, as well as a German word, that has been borrowed by many different nations. German children often attend kindergarten between the ages of three and six. There, they learn to play together and to express themselves clearly and creatively. Kindergarten is not officially a part of Germany's public school system. Parents usually decide whether their children will attend. The overwhelming majority of German children do. Kindergarten classes are run by local governments, churches, private companies, and other groups. Parents often pay all or much of the cost of running the school.

THE PUBLIC SCHOOL SYSTEM

All German children begin attending primary school (*Grundschule*) when they are six years old. In most parts of the

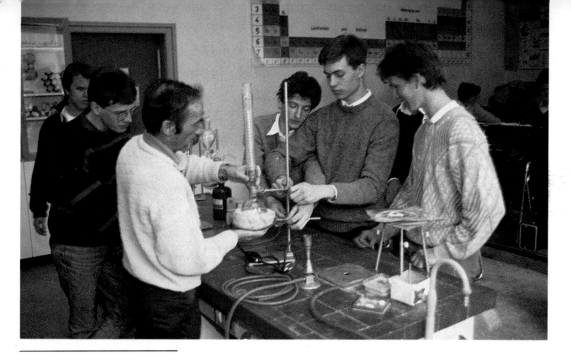

A Gymnasium science class

nation, primary school lasts four years. After that, students, in consultation with parents and teachers, must decide which of three different types of education they want to receive.

Nearly a third of German children choose to attend a type of secondary school (*Hauptschule*), between the ages of 10 and 15. This school teaches academic subjects but also prepares children to begin their working lives.

After completing primary school, some students begin studying at a different secondary school called a *Realschule*. After about six years, although it varies from state to state, students earn a degree a bit more advanced than Hauptschule students. Both groups generally continue their education in vocational schools.

Another type of school is called a *gymnasium*. During their early years at a gymnasium, pupils normally begin to concentrate their studies in one or more specialized areas. Many students who attend a gymnasium eventually plan to attend a university. Typically, it takes nine years to graduate from a gymnasium, the longest course of all German secondary schools.

In recent years, some people have complained about the German public education system. In it, students who are just nine or ten years old must begin making decisions that will shape their adult lives. It is far too easy, some people say, to make a wrong choice that is difficult to change. Because of these criticisms, a fourth type of secondary school, called a comprehensive school (*Gesamtschule*), has become increasingly popular. Comprehensive schools combine the features of the other three types of schools, allowing students to make decisions about their lives when they are a bit more mature.

VOCATIONAL SCHOOLS

The majority of German students attend a vocational institute following their graduation from secondary school. Vocational schools and the apprenticeship system prepare many young people for work in various trades. The most popular German trades are construction workers; cleaning contractors; motor mechanics; bakers; butchers; barbers and hairdressers; cabinetmakers; painters; electricians; plumbers; metalworkers; and radio, television, and computer technicians. There are nearly four hundred other jobs for which training is usually offered. At the same time they prepare for the working world, vocational students take courses such as history and politics.

Most vocational students attend school only a few days a week. On the other days, they work as apprentices, a sort of assistant. Apprentices work with professionals to get on-the-job training in their chosen field. Apprentices are paid for their work. Wages are usually very low at first, but gradually increase. Many vocational

Heidelberg University (left) is located in the center of the city, while the castle is on a slope above the town.

students work as apprentices for two, three, or even four years before completing their educations. Many vocational schools are run by state governments. Large companies often sponsor schools specializing in a specific industry as well.

UNIVERSITIES

Most of the universities in Germany are operated by governments of the sixteen states. Some are extremely old. The University of Heidelberg, for example, was founded in 1386. Quite a few others are also more than five hundred years old. In almost all cases, students must first graduate from a gymnasium before entering a university. University students study advanced subjects in the fields of law, social studies, engineering, humanities, art, mathematics, science, and medicine.

Whether they attend vocational schools or universities, most German men and women eventually begin working, often even before their schooling is completed. Partly because of unification, some jobs in Germany are more difficult to find, even for university graduates.

Munich's BMW administrative offices (left) and museum (bottom of picture); Berlin's International Congress Center (right)

GERMANY'S POWERFUL ECONOMY

Even as a part of a divided nation, the economy of old West Germany was one of the world's strongest. During the 1980s, for example, only Japan and the United States produced more automobiles than West Germany. East Germany also enjoyed some economic success, although it paled in comparison to West Germany. Of all the Communist countries of Eastern Europe, East Germany's economy was the strongest throughout the 1980s.

Many of the products made in Germany are exported to other nations. In 1990, eastern and western Germany together exported goods worth 457 billion dollars in United States money. In recent years West Germany, the United States, and Japan were the top three exporting countries in the world.

In the early 1990s, the German economy was weakened by the expense of unification and by a nearly worldwide recession. The German government was forced to borrow large amounts of money and to raise taxes to have the funds needed to help people hurt by high unemployment rates. At the same time, many German industries were spending large amounts of money to cut back on pollution. Factories in former East German territory also needed cash to modernize their plants to compete successfully in an open market.

THE RUHR VALLEY

An area near the Ruhr River, which empties into the Rhine north of Düsseldorf, has more large factories than any similar-sized place on earth. Cities and towns, inhabited by people who work in the factories, are crowded into the area. Outside of a few city centers, the Ruhr Valley is the most densely populated district in Germany.

It is easy to understand why this area has been such an industrial powerhouse. Enormous deposits of both coal and iron ore are found throughout the Ruhr region. In huge refineries, coal is burned in white-hot blast furnaces, where iron is changed to steel. Nearby factories shape the steel into parts for automobiles, skyscrapers, furniture—almost everything imaginable. With coal and iron ore so close at hand, the refineries and factories of the Ruhr can make finished goods without having to pay expensive transportation fees.

The Ruhr is a nearly ideal place for heavy industry. The area is crisscrossed with canals and train lines. Heavy products can be

A steel worker (above) wears heat-protective clothing; a thermoelectric plant in the Ruhr region (right)

moved cheaply. On the Ruhr River, barges and other ships carry the region's industrial output directly to the Rhine. From there, they go on to the North Sea, the Atlantic Ocean, and the ports of the world.

About one-third of the factories in the Ruhr region were destroyed during World War II. After the war, Allied nations demolished all the surviving factories that had made war materials. They also limited the output of many others. But Germans quickly rebuilt the plants that had been wrecked. By the late 1950s, the Ruhr Valley was producing more material than ever before. Today, the region produces many chemical and textile products in addition to metal and steel parts. Much of the electricity used in western Germany is produced by coal-burning generators in the Ruhr Valley.

INDUSTRIES LARGE AND SMALL

Two of Germany's largest industrial companies produce automobiles. Daimler-Benz AG, headquartered in Stuttgart,

A hand-carved German clock (left) and the Volkswagen factory in Wolfsburg

employs more than 320,000 people worldwide to produce renowned Mercedes-Benz cars and other products. Volkswagenwerk AG, based in Wolfsburg, uses nearly as many employees to make and distribute Volkswagens, small cars noted for their low cost and fuel efficiency. Some other famous German corporations are Siemens AG and Bosch GmbH, producers of electrical components, and the enormous chemical producers BASF and Bayer AG.

Of course, not all of Germany's products are made by huge corporations. There are smaller factories that make, for example, Germany's famous cuckoo clocks. A small number of craftspeople still work in their homes and in little shops to make one-of-a-kind souvenirs and pieces of art. Elaborate wood carvings, for example, are made by skilled Bavarians and sold throughout the world. Largely because of the power of personal computers and

A crowded beer hall during the Oktoberfest in Munich

communication devices, some Germans who used to work in offices are now spending all or part of their time working at home.

In some ways, German industry is changing. Many of the largest factories are still in the Ruhr region, but new areas are developing their own economic muscles. In Stuttgart and some other cities, new high-tech factories have sprung up to develop parts for computers and electronic devices. Although reunification costs weakened Berlin's position as an industrial center, its position should be gradually strengthened again in years to come.

Some of the most famous medium-sized industrial plants in Germany are breweries. In earlier years, there were literally thousands of German breweries. Today, many have gone out of business or have been purchased by larger companies. More than twelve hundred remain, however, to satisfy the nation's unquenchable taste for beer. There are more breweries in Germany than in all other European nations combined. The average German drinks more beer than anyone else in the world.

Vineyards along the Mosel River, like this one, grow white grapes used to produce white wine.

Wine is also a popular drink. Many vineyards—where the grapes that produce wine are grown—can be found in southwestern Germany, especially near the Rhine, Neckar, and Mosel rivers. Grapes have been grown in this area for thousands of years, reflecting the ancient Roman influence.

AGRICULTURE

More than three-fourths of the food eaten in Germany is grown or raised within the nation's borders. The major crops are wheat and other cereals, potatoes, beets and other vegetables, and fruits. Animals used for food, including chickens, pigs, and cattle, are raised on farms.

The question of farm ownership created serious problems when the two Germanys were united. In Communist East Germany, there was no such thing as a private or family-owned farm. All farms were owned by the government or by groups of people—

called collectives—organized by the government. In West Germany, however, most farms were (and still are) owned by private companies or families.

Germans hope that all farms in former East German territories can be turned over to companies and families. However, it is often difficult to decide who owned a farm years ago. Decades earlier, property throughout East Germany, including farmland, was taken away from individual people by the Communist government. To make matters even more difficult, land was illegally taken away from German families by the government of Adolf Hitler more than half a century ago.

Even after all these years, the German government is trying to return all property, including farmlands, to its rightful owners. The process is extremely difficult. By March 1991, nearly half a year after unification took place, approximately 3,500 private farms had been established on former East German territory. In former West German territory, more than 600,000 independent farms already existed.

MILITARY

In the 1950s, because of the fear for the safety of West European nations due to Soviet military buildup, the Allies reversed the policy made at the end of World War II that forbade West Germany to maintain armed forces. Under a task force overseeing the process, West Germany went from demilitarization to rearmament following the added article to the constitution: "The Federation shall build up Armed Forces for defense purposes." East Germany, under Soviet direction, maintained an extensive military and police force.

Part of the aircraft display in the Deutsches Museum in Munich

The *Bundeswehr* (Federal Army) now consists of three branches—the army, air force, and navy. Young German men, from the age of nineteen to twenty-five, are conscripted (drafted) for a military service term of twelve months. The government tries to assign conscripts to duties in accordance with educational and vocational backgrounds and the results of an aptitude test. About half of the armed forces are filled by conscripts; the other half are career servicemen or volunteers; civic service is an alternative for those who do not wish to serve in the armed forces.

A North Sea fisherman and a couple in Berlin (above);
traditional southern German outfits (below)

Chapter 9

LIFE AMONG

THE GERMANS

As a people, Germans often are portrayed by describing their differences. Plenty of political boundaries existed in the past to keep them apart, free to develop their own regional personalities. Cultural differences caused by the division between old West Germany and East Germany are still very noticeable. But there is a north and south division that is perhaps even stronger and certainly far older. In the past, for example, the Bavarians of the south were often bitter enemies of the Prussians to the north. A few of these old rivalries remain.

Whether it is based on truth or colorful fiction, Germans themselves often stereotype people from the various regions. Rhinelanders, who live along the Rhine River near Belgium and France, are said to be good-natured and easy to get along with. The southern Bavarians, people often say, are lively and excitable. Frisians, who live in northernmost Germany between the North and Baltic seas, supposedly speak very little and are sometimes considered unsophisticated. Broad descriptions like these go on and on.

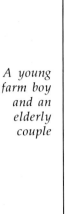

A young farm boy and an elderly couple

There is no doubt that, in their patterns of speech, Germans certainly vary a great deal. Differences are so great, in fact, that a person from one region sometimes has difficulty understanding a speaker from another, even though their written language is the same.

These matters are not quite as simple as they seem. During the final years of World War II, and for several more years after the war, many Germans and other Europeans lost their homes and were forced to move, sometimes great distances. World War II refugees brought their regional traits to their new locations. Traditional regional patterns were somewhat broken up by the war, as well as by the normal movement of people in happier times.

Regardless of the region a German lives in, it is possible to travel to another area in record time.

LIFE IN THE FAST LANE

German cities and towns are connected by one of the most modern and efficient transportation systems in the world.

Traveling on the Autobahn, the vast motorway network that was begun during the Nazi period

Lufthansa, the country's famous airline, has flights between many German cities and to virtually all parts of the globe as well. Lufthansa and other airlines bring many foreign visitors to Germany. In recent years, the country has become the most popular tourist stop in Europe after England.

Germany's national railway is named *Deutsche Bundesbahn*, but most Germans merely call it the "DB." It is one of the most extensive and reliable rail systems in Europe. All major intercity trains have full-menu restaurant cars. Most have traveling snack vendors as well.

Probably the most famous parts of the German transportation system are the superhighways, the Autobahnen, that link most major cities. On lanes of the Autobahnen, there is no speed limit whatsoever. Automobiles can sometimes be seen driving 125 miles per hour (200 kilometers per hour) on these efficient highways. At such high speeds, it is possible to drive from

Germany's northern border to its southernmost cities in nine hours or less. German highways are fast, but they are also controversial. There is talk about the number of fatalities on the Autobahnen and much concern about the impact of the auto emissions on the environment.

In general, roads in former East German territories are not as good as in old West German states. New road construction projects should soon help people from eastern Germany join their western cousins in the fast lanes. The citizens from old East Germany appear all too ready to do just that. Traffic accidents in former East German territories were 75 percent higher in 1990 than in the previous year.

JOURNEY'S END

Fast-traveling Germans have many places to visit in their leisure time, and they enjoy more time off than many other groups of people. In many German companies, the trend is toward a work week just thirty-five hours long. Many German workers get paid vacations totaling at least six weeks during the year.

During the summer, vacationers flock to the beaches of the North and Baltic seas. Hill and mountain areas from the Black Forest and the Bavarian Alps in the south to the Harz Mountains in central Germany attract both winter skiers and summer sightseers. All of Germany's major cities, and many of its smaller towns, have museums, concerts, cultural exhibits, seasonal festivals, and historic sites that attract German and foreign visitors alike.

At least in western Germany, people seldom have to travel very

In summer, vacationers flock to the mountains and beaches of Germany.

far to reach a gambling casino run by one of the various state governments. In a casino, gamblers can feed coins to slot machines or put their chips down on poker and roulette tables to try their luck and perhaps win some money. Most casinos require men to wear jackets and ties—and many males wear tuxedos instead. Women are often dressed in designer gowns.

Since unification, a new dimension has been added to German travel. For the first time, people in eastern Germany are free to visit relatives in western Germany and to become first-time tourists in their own land. For everyone, east-west travel is far easier than in the days of the old Iron Curtain. Many Germans are using their leisure time to discover parts of their country that political squabbles once prevented them from seeing.

THE SPORTING LIFE

For decades, athletes from the old German Democratic Republic won far more Olympic medals than contestants from any other

Germans are avid soccer fans and players.

relatively small nation. During the years Germany was a divided nation, athletic clubs, organized for children, teenagers, and adults as well, were important features on both sides of the Iron Curtain. Their significance continues today. About one-third of all Germans belong to at least one sports club. The most popular matches are in the sports of soccer (called football or *Fussball* in German), gymnastics, tennis, and marksmanship. In former East German states, fishing clubs rival soccer organizations in popularity. Of course, some people participate in sporting and athletic events without belonging to organized clubs. Many golfers and outdoor hikers, for example, do not belong to organized clubs.

Cycling clubs have relatively few members, but the numbers can be misleading. For exercise, fun, and inexpensive travel, far more Germans ride bicycles regularly than people in many other countries. By a narrow margin, more German households own at least one bicycle than own one or more cars.

TELEVISION AND MOVIES

During the days of the Weimar Republic in the 1920s and early 1930s, German cinema enjoyed a golden age. Films by directors such as Fritz Lang, Ernst Lubitsch, and others attracted international audiences. With Hitler's rise to power, however, international acclaim for German cinema declined. Many people involved in the motion picture industry fled to other nations. After the war, it took nearly twenty years for the German film business to develop serious new talents. But Germany's golden age of movies never really returned. In fact, cinema ticket sales have declined steadily for more than thirty years.

Most German moviemakers admit that their industry has been in a crisis. Back in 1956, West German movie houses sold more than 820 million tickets. By 1985, nearly thirty years later, only 104 million tickets were sold. During that period, half the movie houses in the nation were forced to close. Cinema attendance in East Germany also declined during the same era. At the end of that period, in 1985, the average East German spent 7½ hours each year in a movie house, and more than 750 hours watching television.

The popularity of television is one reason for Germany's declining theatrical film business. Today, VCRs and cable TV hookups are becoming more numerous throughout the nation. In 1990, about half of all former West German households owned VCRs, although the percentage is much lower in areas that were once part of East Germany. After World War II, German filmmakers found it difficult to compete in their own country with motion pictures produced in Hollywood. Many American films were written according to formulas guaranteed to please the

Informal or formal, Germans love classical music.

widest possible audience. Some of the best German directors and screenwriters, who refused to follow Hollywood's lead, suffered disastrous economic consequences. Despite the best efforts of a new generation of filmmakers, more and more German movies will probably be made specifically for television in the future.

PERFORMING ARTS

It should come as no surprise that the land of Bach, Beethoven, and Wagner still has an active classical music scene. There are more than 150 symphony orchestras in Germany. Some people believe that the Berlin Philharmonic, formerly led by Herbert von Karajan and then by Claudio Abado, is the best orchestra in the world. The Gewandhaus Orchestra of Leipzig, the Munich Philharmonic, and the Bamberg Symphony also are highly regarded.

In July, opera lovers flock to the little town of Bayreuth, where Richard Wagner once lived and worked. During most summers since 1876, the annual Bayreuth Wagner festival has attracted

The opera house in Bayreuth is the best-preserved Baroque theater in Germany.

thousands of people for its highly regarded opera performances. At other times, the operatic focus shifts to Munich and Hamburg. Permanent opera companies, as well as other musical stage productions, can be found in Berlin and other leading German cities as well. Ballet performances center around the cities of Berlin, Hamburg, and Stuttgart.

As in other nations, jazz, pop, and rock musicians are very popular in Germany, especially among young people. Performances by these musicians take place almost anywhere, from huge sports arenas to smaller concert halls and to even more intimate nightclubs. Very few German rock-and-roll stars are known outside of Europe.

About 20 million people attend live theater performances in Germany each year. Most theater-goers, up to 90 percent in some places, buy what are called subscription tickets from theater organizations. The largest and oldest of these groups, the *Volksbühne*, "People's Stage," has a quarter of a million members.

A scene from the Passion Play performed every ten years at Oberammergau

The usual subscription season includes performances of ten to twelve different plays. Largely because of these groups, Germany's live theater industry is in better financial health than its film business.

GERMANY'S CHANGING DIET

Think of German food. Do images of sauerkraut, sausages, potatoes, and rich desserts come to mind? They are all popular German foods, but not all are equally fashionable everywhere in the country. Like so much else in German life, what people eat often depends on where they live.

More than seven hundred years ago, cities in the Hanseatic League made fortunes trading herring. Today, herring—pickled, smoked, marinated, or fresh—is still a popular dish in northern Germany. So are eels and a wide variety of Atlantic fish. But to the south, along the Rhine Valley and eastward into Bavaria, meats

German bratwursts and sausages are well known throughout Europe and North America. Herring sandwiches and elaborate sundaes are very popular with Germans.

such as smoked ham, pickled beef, roasted oxen, and a wide variety of sausages are more often served.

Traditionally, most German diets are high in starch. The ever-present noodles and dumplings of southern dishes are often replaced by potatoes in the north. One ingredient common in almost all German diets is bread. In many delicious sizes, shapes, and forms, Germans, at least in the past, ate bread at almost every meal. A snack made up of grilled wurst sausages served on a bun can be found in just about any German city or town.

Take a diet high in fatty meats and starches, wash it down with plenty of rich German beer, add a delicious dessert made with an abundance of sugar and shortening, and what do you have? The answer is calories, calories, and more calories.

During the 1960s and 1970s, German doctors and health officials began a major campaign to change the dietary habits of people in both East and West Germany. The traditional German

121

A typical German dinner may include cooked vegetables, potatoes, and meat. Germans often eat dinner, their biggest meal, at noon.

diet, they said, sometimes leads to obesity and a variety of health problems. Today, many Germans are attempting to eat more fruits and vegetables and fewer fatty meats and carbohydrates. Some also are trying to cut down on beer, a very fattening drink. But for many Germans, that is simply going too far. Unfortunately, Germany's love affair with beer has a dark side as well. In 1991, the German Ministry of Health listed alcoholism as a leading cause of death, right after smoking.

Like many other modern people, Germans often enjoy foods from other lands. Italian, Chinese, and Middle Eastern restaurants are extremely popular in the larger cities, especially in western Germany. Some Germans travel to neighboring France to enjoy a weekend outing and to sample some delicious French cooking.

Homes vary, from stark modern apartment buildings to quaint village houses.

HOME LIFE

In the Ruhr Valley and other industrial areas, there are still Germans living in homes they built themselves, brick by brick, following the destruction of World War II. For these people, and their children, and for others who spent more money than they had to buy their shelter, the home can become a sacred place. More than most other people, German homeowners tend to stay put.

For many years following the war, there was a severe housing shortage throughout the divided nation. West Germany was the first to recover, but housing costs remained very high. In East Germany, prices were set by the government and were generally lower, at least for the small apartments in which most East Germans lived. Not enough housing units were built to meet the

Children in a typical middle-class apartment; a father and his daughter (left) dressed for Oktoberfest

demand. Young East German families were often put on waiting lists for new housing and stayed on the lists for years. For many young West German families, new houses were easier to find, but difficult to afford. Like their East German cousins, many decided to live in modest apartments.

Today, the residents of former West Germany live comfortably, with homes and labor-saving appliances. Conditions in former East Germany are not as good. When they were running in the 1990 elections, some German politicians claimed that living standards in eastern Germany would match the western part of the nation within five years.

German families tend to be small. For reasons that are not entirely clear, many German couples have decided not to have children at all. For years, the East German government encouraged people to have large families by giving them price

Time together: a family bicycles through the Englischer Garten

breaks for housing. The results were mixed. As a whole, the German nation still has one of the lowest, or possibly the lowest, birthrate in the world.

Some German couples decide not to have children so that both husband and wife can work full time. For these people, a high standard of living is more important than raising a family. Some hard-working Americans are called "Yuppies," who might be compared to some of these hard-working Germans.

Whether they have large or small families, most Germans teach their children to be very polite around company and adults. As they grow a bit older, like other teenagers, many German adolescents rebel against the good manners they were taught. Still, Germans of any age tend to treat their home with considerable care. The price paid to live in it has simply demanded respect.

Woodcarving and flower-adorned houses are traditions in Germany.

A NATION WITH A PAST—AND A FUTURE

In the 1990s, representatives from many nations were finalizing plans for a historic reorganization of European nations. The United States of Europe or the European Community became the European Union (EU) in 1994. The plan calls for removal of most trade barriers between European countries, a single form of money for all member states, and the virtual elimination of travel restrictions throughout much of the continent.

Germany is in a perfect position to play a pivotal role in the creation of a new order in Europe and the world. It has recently experienced the opportunities and problems created by its own

*Continuing traditions while keeping pace
with the future is the task of Germany's youth.*

economic unification. It can surely help other nations by sharing what it has learned. It has also shown great determination in working with the United Nations and other international organizations to help create a world ruled by law. More than most other nations, it has ample evidence of the terrible consequences of international military competition.

From the genius of Beethoven to the madness of Hitler, German culture has brought to the world some of humanity's highest achievements, and a few of its deepest transgressions. This powerful young nation, this rich and ancient culture, is once again whole and free. Better than any other people, Germans should be able to learn from the past and lead the way to a brighter future.

MAP KEY

Aachen	E4	Kassel	E5
Augsburg	F5	Kempten	F5
Baden-Baden	F4	Kiel Kan (canal)	C4, C5
Baltic Sea	C6, B6, B7	Kiel	C5
Bamberg	E5	Koblenz	E4
Bautzen	D6	Landshut	F5
Berlin	D6	Leipzig	D5
Bielefeld	D4	Lubeck	C5
Bohemian Forest (mountains)	E6	Lubecker Bucht (bay)	C5
Bonn	E4	Magdeburg	D5
Brandenburg	D5	Mainz	E4
Braunschweig	D5	Mannheim	E4
Bremen	D4	Munich	F5
Bremerhaven	D4	Münster	D4
Celle	D5	Neumunster	C5
Cologne	E4	Nordhausen	D5
Cottbus	D6	North Frisian Island	C4
Cuxhaven	C4	North Sea	B3, B4, C3, C4, D3, D4
Danube (river)	F5, F6	Nürnberg	E5
Darmstadt	E4	Oder (river)	D6
Dessau	D5	Oldenburg	D4
Dortmund	D4	Passau	F6
Dresden	D6	Pforzheim	F4
Duisburg	D4	Plauen	E5
Düsseldorf	E4	Potsdam	D5
Eisenach	E5	Regensburg	E5
Elbe (river)	D5, D6	Rhein (Rhine) (river)	E4, F4
Erfurt	E5	Rosenheim	F5
Essen	D4	Rostock	C5
Flensburg	C4	Rügen (island)	C6
Frankfurt	E4	Saarbrücken	E4
Freiberg	E6	Schaffhausen	F4
Freiburg	F4	Schleswig	C4
Fulda	E5	Stralsund	C5
Fürth	E5	Stuttgart	F5
Gera	E5	Trier	E4
Gorlitz	D6	Ulm	F5
Gotha	E5	Weimar	E5
Halle	D5	Weser (river)	D4
Hamburg	C5	Wiesbaden	E4
Hannover	D5	Wilhelmshaven	D4
Heidelberg	E4	Wismar	C5
Heilbronn	E5	Worms	E4
Hildesheim	D5	Wuppertal	E4
Inn (river)	F6	Würzburg	E5
Isar (river)	F5, F6	Wurzen	D5
Jena	E5	Zwickau	E5
Kaiserslautern	E4		
Karl-Marx-Stadt	E6		
Karlsruhe	F4		

Continued on pages 160-161

2   3   4   5   6   7   8

A   B   C   D   E   F   G   H

MINI-FACTS AT A GLANCE

GENERAL INFORMATION

Official Name: *Bundesrepublik Deutschland* (Federal Republic of Germany)

Capital: Bonn; Capital designate is Berlin

Official Language: German. At present, the spoken and written form of standard German is based largely on High German, which was spoken originally in the southern and central highlands of Germany. Low German, spoken in the northern plains, can still be heard in some farm areas. In addition, there are many dialects.

Government: Germany is a federal republic. Citizens over the age of eighteen may vote. The legislature is divided into an upper and lower chamber. The *Bundestag,* the lower chamber, has 672 members, all elected to four-year terms. Sixty-eight members of the *Bundesrat,* the upper chamber, are appointed for indefinite terms by the sixteen (ten from West Germany, five from the newly created states of former East Germany, and one from the state of Berlin) *Länder,* or states.

Flag: The flag has three equal horizontal stripes in black, red, and gold.

National Song: Third stanza of *"Deutschland-Lied"* ("Song of Germany")

Religion: There is no official religion. About 49 percent of the Germans are Protestants; most of this group belong to the Lutheran church. Approximately 33 percent of Germans are Roman Catholics, and about 2 percent are Muslims. Some 40,000 Jews live in Germany.

Money: The basic unit is the Deutsche Mark (DM). There are 100 Pfennig (Pf.) to the mark. In November 1995, 1.42 Deutsche Marks equalled one dollar in United States currency.

Membership in International Organizations: European Bank for Reconstruction and Development (EBRD); European Union (EU); Inter-American Development Bank (IDB); International Monetary Fund (IMF); North Atlantic Treaty Organization (NATO); Organization for Economic Cooperation and Development (OECD); United Nations (UN) and its various organizations; West European Union (WEU)

Population: 81,966,000 (1994 estimate); distribution is 85 percent urban, 15 percent rural. The density is 595 persons per sq. mi. (230 persons per sq. km).

Cities:

Berlin	3,465,700
Hamburg	1,688,800
Munich (München)	1,256,600
Cologne (Köln)	960,600
Frankfurt	664,000
Essen	627,300

Dortmund	600,700
Stuttgart	599,400
Düsseldorf	578,100
Bremen	554,400
Hannover	523,600
Leipzig	496,600
Dresden	481,700
Bonn	298,200
Chemnitz	283,600
Magdeburg	279,900
Rostock	248,800

(Population based on 1993 estimates)

GEOGRAPHY

Land Regions: There are four main land regions in Germany. From north to south, they are (1) the Northern Plains, (2) the Central Highlands, (3) the Alpine Foothills, and (4) the Rhine River Valley.

Borders: North—Denmark, the North Sea, the Baltic Sea
      South—Austria, Switzerland
      West—The Netherlands, Belgium, Luxembourg, France
      East—Poland, Czech Republic

Highest point: Zugspitze, 9,721 ft. (2,963 m), in the Alps

Lowest point: Riepsterhammerick, 6.5 ft. (2 m) below sea level on the coast

Rivers: Major rivers include the Danube, Elbe, Neisse, Oder, Peene, Recknitz, Rhine, Saale, Warnow, Werra, and Weser. The Danube is the only major river in Germany that flows eastward. About three-quarters of all waterway freight is carried on the Rhine.

Lakes: Many lakes found throughout Germany were formed by ancient glaciers from the Alps.

Mountains: The Bavarian Alps, part of the largest mountain system in Europe, rise more than 6,000 ft. (1,829 m). The Schwarzwald is also a mountainous region; its average peaks rise between 2,500 and 3,000 ft. (762 and 914 m), with some as high as 4,000 ft. (1,219 m). The South German hills rise from about 500 to 2,500 ft. (152 to 762 m). The Thuringer Wald mountains is south central Germany are popular vacation spots. The Erzgebirge along the Czech Republic border reach elevations up to 4,770 ft. (1,454 m).

Forests: Forests cover nearly 30 percent of Germany. Two-thirds of the forests consist of firs, pines, spruces, and other cone-bearing trees. Other trees include beeches, birches, and oaks.

Climate: The climate is mild. The average temperature in January, the coldest month, is about 30° F. (–1° C). The hottest month, July, has an average temperature of 65° F. (18° C). There are approximately 20 to 40 in. (51 to 102 cm) of precipitation a year, most of which falls during the summer growing season.

Greatest Distances: North to South: 540 mi. (869 km)
East to West: 392 mi. (631 km)
Coastline: 574 mi. (924 km)

Area: 137,854 sq. mi. (357,042 sq. km)

ECONOMY AND INDUSTRY

Principal Products:
Agriculture: Beef and dairy cattle, sheep, hogs, poultry, dairy products, potatoes, barley, oats, rye, sugar beets, wheat, apples, and grapes (for wine making)
Fishing: Shrimp, cod, herring, mackerel, and redfish
Manufacturing: Iron and steel, automobiles, trucks, locomotives and ships, cement, clothing, electric equipment, processed foods, beer, metal, cameras, computers, leather goods, scientific instruments, machinery, chemicals, fertilizers, drugs, plastics, toys, wood pulp, and paper
Mining: Coal, iron ore, lead, petroleum, rock salt, zinc, copper, tin, uranium, and potash

Communication: There are about 400 daily newspapers. The *Bild-Zeitung* of Hamburg has been largest. About 12,500 different magazines are published in Germany. Most German homes have a radio and more than half have a television set. Radio and television programming is produced for the most part by public corporations. Commercials are broadcast at only a few special times during the day. Everyone who owns a radio or television set must pay a monthly license fee to support the networks. Cable television is a growing industry. The postal, telegraph, and telephone systems are owned by the government.

Transportation: The railroad, owned by the government, is being privatized, and consists of about 56,813 mi. (91,432 km) of track, which connects all parts of Germany. There are also approximately 395,400 mi. (636,300 km) of roads across Germany. This includes 5,100 mi. (8,207 km) of four-lane superhighways known as *Autobahnen.* There is no speed limit on the Autobahnen. Germany have about 33 million automobiles, 1.8 million buses, trucks, and other commercial vehicles. The Rhine River and its branches are extremely important in water transportation. Virtually all major rivers are connected by a system of man-made canals. The seagoing merchant fleet is made up of about 1,700 ships. Hamburg and Bremen are the major seaports. Deutsche Lufthansa is the government-owned airline. There are some 40 commercial airports in Germany.

EVERYDAY LIFE

Food: The main meal in Germany, generally served at noon, might consist of veal or pork and vegetables such as beets, carrots, onions, potatoes, or turnips. A soft-boiled egg, rolls, and jam, served with coffee or milk, usually make up a breakfast. A light supper, served in the evening, might consist of bread, cheese, and sausage. There is a trend toward low-fat, healthier—even macro-biotic—diets and international cuisine, especially in urban areas. German beer and wine are world-famous for their high quality. Some popular German food items are sauerkraut, sauerbraten, bratwurst, frankfurters, and limburger and Münster cheese.

Housing: Germany suffers from a housing shortage and rents remain high. Most people live in apartments. Few people own homes, since land is very expensive. There is a long waiting period for apartment occupancy.

Holidays: Official holidays include New Year's Day, Good Friday, Easter, Pentecost, Labor Day (May 1), and Christmas. In Catholic areas, the Feast of Corpus Christi (celebrated eleven days after Pentecost) and All Saints' Day (November 1) are important events. Lutheran areas celebrate Reformation Day (October 31) and Repentance and Prayer Day (third Wednesday in November). In addition, many cities have various feasts and festivals.

Culture: German has more than 200 theaters and opera houses, about 100 large orchestras, and more than 2,000 museums. Most of the theaters and opera houses rely on subsidies from the state and local governments. German music and drama festivals are praised throughout the world for their quality. Some of the best known are the Bayreuth Festival, featuring Wagner's music, and jazz festivals in Berlin. Nearly 70,000 new books are published each year. Popular writers often have their works translated. As an example, Nobel Prize winner Heinrich Böll's writings have been translated into thirty-five languages.

Music: Johann Sebastian Bach and George Frederick Handel established the great tradition of German music in the early 1700s. Later the tradition was carried on by such famous composers as Wolfgang Amadeus Mozart, Ludwig van Beethoven, Felix Mendelssohn, Franz Schubert, Richard Wagner, and Kurt Weill. In the end of the twentieth century, folk music by Wolf Biermann and Hannes Wader, and rock and new-wave music of Udo Lindenberg and Nina Hagen became popular.

Sports and Recreation: The most popular sport in Germany is soccer, called *Fussball.* Sharpshooting, gymnastics, tennis, and track also are popular. Other favorite activities include hiking, canoeing, rowing, sailing, and swimming. Skiing is a favorite winter sport. Inexpensive inns called Youth Hostels are popular with young Germans.

Schools: Education is free and is controlled by the state government. Every child between the ages of six and sixteen must attend school. All children spend four years at primary school (*Grundschule*), followed by five years at secondary school (*Hauptschule*), six years at intermediate school (*Realschule*), or nine years at high school (*Gymnasium*). Pupils finishing secondary school usually become apprentices for three years so they can learn a trade. Intermediate school helps young people prepare for jobs in business and administration. A small number of *Gesamtschulen* (comprehensive schools) operate as alternatives to the other three divisions of school. The graduation certificate (*Abitur*) from Gymnasium qualifies a student for university studies. There are about 250 universities and other institutions of higher learning in Germany, as well as more than twenty-five art and music academies. The total student population at colleges and universities numbers nearly 2 million and includes more than 55,000 foreign students. Tuition is free. In the early 1990s, the literacy rate was about 99 percent.

Health: German people in general enjoy good health and have access to modern health facilities. They have comprehensive health insurance coverage. Sickness insurance pays for all medical attention. In the early 1990s, there were 310 persons per doctor, 1,400 persons per dentist, and 125 persons per hospital bed. Life expectancy at 73 years for males and 80 years for females is high. Infant mortality rate at 6 per 1,000 live births is low.

Social Welfare: Germany has an extensive system of social security and welfare. It covers old-age pensions, unemployment and sickness benefits, allowances for injury, rent, and child care, as well as grants for education and job training. About one-third of the gross national product is spent on social security.

IMPORTANT DATES

1000 B.C.—Tribes from northern Europe begin to arrive in present-day Germany

A.D. 9—German tribes defeat Roman General Varus at the Battle of Teutoburg Forest

12—Romans build Castra Bonnensia, which becomes the city of Bonn

50—Cologne becomes a resort for Roman veterans

179—Regensburg is founded

259—Franks cross the Rhine River

742—Birth of Charlemagne

800—Charlemagne is crowned "Emperor of the Romans"

814—Charlemagne dies

843—Treaty of Verdun; empire divided among Lothair (Central Empire), Charles the Bald (Western Empire), and Louis the German (Eastern Empire)

845—Hamburg is destroyed by Vikings

870—Cologne's first cathedral is built

911—The last of Charlemagne's heirs dies; First German monarchy established; Conrad I of Franconia elected king

919—Henry I of Saxony becomes king of Germans

962—Holy Roman Empire established; Otto the Great crowned

1156—Frederick I named emperor; Holy Roman Empire strongest ever

1372—Frankfurt becomes a free city

1386—University of Heidelberg founded

1400s—Reformation movement begins in Bohemia

1438—Hapsburg family of Austria begins almost continuous rule of Holy Roman Empire

1445—Johannes Gutenberg perfects letterpress printing

1483—Birth of Martin Luther

1493—Peasants' Revolt

1517—Luther nails up his complaints about the church to the cathedral door in Wittenberg; Reformation begins in Germany

1524—War of the Peasants

1555—Religious Peace of Augsburg legalizes Lutheran-Roman Catholic split

1582—Würzburg University founded

1618-48—Thirty Years' War

1648—Hapsburgs defeated; Treaty of Westphalia ends Thirty Years' War; Austria breaks from the empire

1701—Brandenburg-Prussia becomes the independent kingdom of Prussia; Berlin Academy of Sciences founded

1749-86—Frederick the Great consolidates Prussia; makes it a great power

1749—Poet Johann Wolfgang von Goethe born

1806—Napoleon invades, ends the Holy Roman Empire

1812—Brothers Grimm begin collecting fairy tales

1813—Napoleon is defeated at Leipzig

1815—Congress of Vienna establishes the German Confederation with 39 sovereign states; Otto von Bismarck is born

1824—Ludwig van Beethoven composes his Ninth Symphony

1833—German Customs Union (the *Zollverein*) founded

1848—Revolution throughout Europe; German Confederation ends; Karl Marx finishes his "Communist Manifesto"; German national parliament is established at Frankfurt

1849—Thousands of German republicans emigrate to the United States

1850—German Confederation is refounded

1856—Discovery of Neanderthal man skeleton near Düsseldorf

1862—Bismarck is named premier of Prussia

1864—Prussia defeats Denmark

1866—Prussia defeats Austria, establishes the North German Federation; Bismarck named federal chancellor

1871—Prussia and German states defeat France; German Empire (the *Reich*) is founded

1876—Nikolaus Otto creates the first modern auto engine; inauguration of the Bayreuth Festival

1878—Albert Einstein is born

1882—Germany, Austria, Hungary, and Italy form an alliance against Russia's influence in the Middle East and the Balkans

1885–Karl Benz builds the first automobile

1890–Bismarck is ousted as chancellor

1914-18–World War I; Allies defeat Central Powers; German Empire is ended

1919–Treaty of Versailles signed in France; Weimar Republic formed

1921–Albert Einstein wins Nobel Prize in physics

1925–Paul von Hindenburg is named Reich president

1932–Six million Germans are unemployed

1933–Adolf Hitler is named Reich chancellor and becomes dictator; Parliament
is disbanded; Hitler proclaims the *Third Reich* (1934-1945); Einstein emigrates to
America

1936–Olympic games in Berlin

1938–Austria is annexed by Germany, along with German-speaking areas of
Sudetenland from Czechoslovakia

1939–Germany and Soviet Union sign a non-aggression pact

1939-45–World War II; Allies defeat Germany; Hitler commits suicide

1945–Germany is divided into four military occupation zones under Potsdam
Conference provisions

1947–Mass expulsion of Germans from Eastern Europe

1948–Berlin blockade and airlift; Marshall Plan launched

1949–Federal Republic of Germany is founded; Theodor Heuss is named first
federal president; Konrad Adenauer is named federal chancellor; NATO is
founded; German Democratic Republic is founded; Wilhelm Pieck is elected
president

1953–Revolt in the German Democratic Republic is crushed by Soviet tanks

1954–Soviet Union grants complete sovereignty to East Germany

1955–West Germany and East Germany are declared independent countries;
West Germany becomes a member of NATO; the Warsaw Pact is formed with the
Soviet Union, East Germany, Poland, Czechoslovakia, Hungary, Romania,
Bulgaria, and Albania

1957–The Treaty of Rome creates the European Economic Community with
France, West Germany, Italy, The Netherlands, Belgium, and Luxembourg as
members; French-controlled Saarland rejoins West Germany as its 10th state

1958–Soviet Union demands the withdrawal of Western troops from Berlin

1961–Berlin Wall is erected

1963–Ludwig Erhard is named chancellor of West Germany

1964–Willi Stoph is elected East German premier

1966–Kurt Kiesinger is named chancellor of West Germany; diplomatic
relations are established with Romania

1968–New East German constitution revokes some civil rights contained in
1949 charter; East German forces participate in the Soviet-bloc invasion of
Czechoslovakia

1969–Witty Brandt is named chancellor of West Germany

1971–Brandt receives Nobel Peace Prizes; Eric Honecker replaces Walter Ulbricht as East German Socialist Unity party's chief secretary

1972–Olympic games are held in Munich; West Germany and East Germany sign a treaty recognizing each other's sovereignty

1973–Treaty between East and West Germany is ratified; treaty signed with Czechoslovakia; Federal Republic and German Democratic Republic become members of the United Nations

1974–West German government passed the Federal Emission Protection Act to help clean the air; Helmut Schmidt named chancellor of West Germany; World Cup soccer championships are held in Munich

1976–Eric Honecker replaces Willi Stoph as East German head of state

1979–Karl Carstens is elected West Germany's fifth president

1980–Peace demonstrations continue across West Germany

1981–Martial law is declared in Poland

1982–Helmut Kohl becomes chancellor of West Germany

1983–The environmentalist party, the Greens, win seats in the *Bundestag* for the first-time

1984–Dr. Richard von Weizsäcker is elected West Germany's sixth president

1985–Mikhail Gorbachev becomes Soviet leader who wants to change government through *perestroika* (reconstruction) and *glasnost* (openness)

1987–Elections take place in January; the Greens again win seats in the *Bundestag*; a young German, Mathias Rust, flies a solo light aircraft from Finland to Moscow, undetected by Soviet defenses; Erich Honecker visits West Germany; Rudolf Hess, the last Nazi war prisoner, dies at Spandau jail in West Berlin

1989–Hungary opens its border with Austria, allowing East Germans to stream out; Erich Honecker is ousted from East Germany's Communist leadership and is succeeded by Egon Krenz; on November 9 the Berlin Wall officially opens and all travel restrictions are lifted; European summit meeting in Strasbourg

1990–East Germany formally withdraws from the Soviet-led Warsaw Pact and Soviet President Gorbachev allows new Germany to become a member of NATO; World War II allied powers and East and West Germany sign Final Settlement granting full sovereignty to a unified Germany; at the stroke of midnight on October 3, East Germany ceases to exist; both Germanys are united under Article 23 of West Germany's constitution to form Federal Republic of Germany; Helmut Kohl is elected first chancellor of unified Germany

1991–Berlin is designated as the capital of Federal Republic of Germany; some 21 percent of the former East Germans are estimated to be unemployed; Helmut Kohl is reelected chancellor

1992–The first memorial in Germany specifically honoring Jewish victims of the Holocaust–Wannsee Holocaust Museum–opens

1993 – In the first trial of its kind in Germany, a German court finds three former East German officials guilty of inciting East German border guards to shoot to kill East German citizens fleeing west; the first Jewish high school to open in Germany since the Holocaust reopens in central Berlin; Germany suffers the worst economic recession since World War II

1994 – Roman Herzog is the first elected federal president since unification; Kohl plans that Germany will push to open the European Union (EU) to Eastern European nations when Germany takes over rotating presidency of the EU later in 1994; Helmut Kohl is reelected for his fourth term as Chancellor; Erich Honecker, former communist leader of East Germany, dies in Santiago, Chile; Germany assumes the rotating EU presidency for six months

1995 – United Nation's climactic conference is held in Berlin and is attended by more than 120 countries

IMPORTANT PEOPLE

Konrad Adenauer (1876-1967), chancellor of West Germany, 1949-63

Alfred Andersch (1914-80), novelist who deals with subject of Hitler's rise to power

Johann Sebastian Bach (1685-1750), composer

Ernst Barlach (1870-1938), artist, sculptor, playwright, and poet

Max Beckmann (1799-1859), landscape and architectural painter

Ludwig van Beethoven (1770-1827), composer, born in Bonn

Otto von Bismarck (1815-98), Prussian statesman, first chancellor of German Empire

Gebhard von Blücher (1742-1819), Prussian field marshal

Heinrich Böll (1917-85), novelist and poet, received Nobel Prize in literature in 1972

Johannes Brahms (1833-97), composer and pianist, born in Hamburg

Willy Brandt (1913-92), mayor of West Berlin, 1957-66; chancellor of West Germany, 1969-74; winner of 1971 Nobel Peace Prize

Bertolt Brecht (1889-1956), playwright and poet, in exile from 1935

Karl Carstens (1914-92), president of West Germany, 1979-84

Charles IV (1316-78), crowned Holy Roman Emperor in 1355; issued Golden Bull in 1356

Karl von Clausewitz (1780-1831), Prussian army officer known for books on science of war, born in Burg

Karl Dönitz (1891-1981), naval commander who planned and commanded U-boat fleet; sentenced as war criminal

Albrecht Dürer (1471-1528), painter and engraver

Ludwig Erhard (1897-1977), economist and politician; chancellor of West Germany, 1963-66

Wolfram von Eschenbach (1170-1220), medieval poet who wrote *Parsifal*

Rainer Werner Fassbinder (1946-82), filmmaker

Johann Gottlieb Fichte (1762-1814), philosopher and metaphysician

Marie Luise Fleiber (1901-74), playwright

Theodor Fontane (1819-98), poet, novelist, and essayist

Frederick I., Barbarossa (1123?-1190), Holy Roman emperor, 1152-90

Frederick William (1620-88), elector of Brandenburg

Paul J. Goebbels (1897-1945), official propagandist of Germany, committed suicide

Hermann W. Goering (1893-1946), second in command to Adolf Hitler in Nazi Germany, committed suicide

Johann Wolfgang von Goethe (1749-1832), Romantic poet, born at Frankfurt am Main

Günter Grass (1927-   ), novelist and poet, who dealt with subject of Hitler era

Walter Gropius (1883-1969), architect who founded the Bauhaus school to coordinate the building arts

Mattias Grünewald (1465?-1528), painter regarded as greatest representative of German Gothic style

Johannes Gutenberg (?-1468), inventor of first modern printing press, born in Mainz

George Frederick Handel (1685-1759), composer, born in Halle

Gerhart Hauptmann (1862-1946), writer and playwright, received Nobel Prize in literature in 1912

Franz Joseph Haydn (1732-1809), German poet and composer

Georg Wilhelm Hegel (1770-1831), philosopher, born in Stuttgart

Heinrich Heine (1797-1856), lyric poet and literary critic

Herman Hesse (1877-1962), German novelist, received 1946 Nobel Prize for literature

Rudolf Hess (1893-1987), Nazi politician sentenced as war criminal; died at Spandau jail

Paul von Hindenburg (1847-1934), general during World War I; president of Weimar Republic, 1925-34; born in Posen

Adolf Hitler (1889-1945), chancellor and dictator, brought on World War II by invading Poland, committed suicide

Rolf Hochhuth (1931-   ), playwright who has dealt with treatment of Jews in World War II

Hans Holbein the Elder (1465?-1524), historical painter

Hans Holbein the Younger (1497?-1524), portrait and historical painter

Erich Honecker (1912-94), head of the state of East Germany, 1976-89

Wilhelm von Humboldt (1767-1835), educational reformer in Prussia

Uwe Johnson (1934-84), novelist during the Communist rule in East Germany

Franz Kafka (1883-1924), poet and novelist, wrote about anxiety and alienation in 20th century

Immanuel Kant (1724-1804), metaphysical and transcendental philosopher

Marie Luise Kaschnitz (1901-74), novelist

Wilhelm Keitel (1882-1946), Nazi field marshal hanged as war criminal

Kurt Georg Kiesinger (1904-88), chancellor of West Germany, 1966-69

Helmut Kohl (1930-   ), chancellor of West Germany, 1982-86, 1987-89, 1990-94; reelected in 1994

Fritz Lang (1890-1976), filmmaker

Gotthold Ephraim Lessing (1729-1781), dramatist and critic

Erich F.W. Ludendorff (1865-1937), general and politician who served during World War I

Martin Luther (1483-1546), father of the Reformation

Rosa Luxemburg (1870-1919), socialist agitator

Heinrich Mann (1871-1950), novelist, essayist, and playwright

Thomas Mann (1875-1955), novelist and essayist

Karl Marx (1818-83), materialist philosopher and social reformer

Angelika Mechtel (1943-   ), contemporary novelist

Felix Mendelssohn (1809-47), composer, pianist, and conductor, born in Hamburg

Ludwig Mies van der Rohe (1886-1969), architect known for his steel-and-glass apartment buildings

Helmuth Karl Von Moltke (1800-91), Prussian military genius important in the building of the German Empire

Wolfgang Amadeus Mozart (1756-91), one of the greatest composers of music

Friedrich Nietzsche (1844-1900), philosopher and poet

Tilman Riemenschneider (1460?-1531), sculptor and wood carver

Friedrich von Schiller (1759-1805), poet and playwright

Helmut Schmidt (1918-   ), chancellor of West Germany, 1975-82

Arthur Schopenhauer (1788-1860), philosopher, expounder of pessimism

Robert Schumann (1810-56), composer

Karl Reichsfreiherr von und zum Stein (1757-1831), statesman and social reformer in Prussia

Gottfried von Strassburg (1170-1220), medieval poet, most famous writing is *Tristan und Isolde*

Richard Strauss (1864-1949), conductor and composer

Walter Ulbricht (1893-1973), leader of Socialist Unity party in GDR, 1950-71; chairman of the Council of State, 1960-71

Rudolf Virchow (1812-1902), Prussian pathologist and political leader

Richard Wagner (1813-83), composer and writer on music

Kurt Weill (1900-50), composer of operas, ballets, and musical comedies

Christoph Martin Wieland (1733-1813), poet, prose writer, and translator

Gabriele Wohmann (1932-   ), novelist

Christa Wolf (1929-   ), novelist, known for work criticizing life under Communist rule

INDEX

Page numbers that appear in boldface type indicate illustrations

143

About the Author

Jim Hargrove has worked as a writer and editor for more than 10 years. After serving as an editorial director for three Chicago-area publishers, he began a career as an independent writer, preparing a series of books for children. He has contributed to works by nearly 20 different publishers. Some of his Childrens Press titles are *Enchantment of the World: Belgium, Mark Twain: The Story of Samuel Clemens, Gateway to Freedom: The Story of the Statue of Liberty and Ellis Island, The Story of the Black Hawk War,* and *Microcomputers at Work.* With his wife and teenage daughter, he lives in a small Illinois town near the Wisconsin border.